dim sum

dim sum

traditional favourites and innovative creations

CHAN CHEN HEI

Marshall Cavendish Cuisine

dim sum

Editor	: Lydia Leong
Designer	: Lynn Chin Nyuk Ling
Photographer	: Edmond Ho
Writer	: Sharon Soh

The publisher wishes to thank **Sia Huat Pte Ltd**, **Life Storey Pte Ltd** and **Barang Barang** for the loan and use of their tableware.

The recipes in this book were created by Chef Chan Chen Hei in collaboration with the dim sum chefs at Chef Chan's Restaurant.

© **2005 Marshall Cavendish International (Asia) Private Limited**
Published by Marshall Cavendish Cuisine
An imprint of Marshall Cavendish International (Asia) Private Limited
A member of Times Publishing Limited
Times Centre, 1 New Industrial Road, Singapore 536196
Tel: (65) 6213 9300   Fax: (65) 6285 4871
E-mail: te@sg.marshallcavendish.com
Online Bookstore: www.marshallcavendish.com/genref

Malaysian Office:
Marshall Cavendish (Malaysia) Sdn Bhd (3024-D)
(General & Reference Publishing)
(Formerly known as Federal Publications Sdn Berhad)
Times Subang, Lot 46, Persiaran Teknologi Subang
Subang Hi-Tech Industrial Park
Batu Tiga, 40000 Shah Alam
Selangor Darul Ehsan, Malaysia
Tel: (603) 5635 2191, 5628 6888   Fax: (603) 5635 2706
E-mail: cchong@my.marshallcavendish.com

National Library Board Singapore Cataloguing in Publication Data

Chan, Chen Hei.
Dim sum : traditional favourites and innovative creations / Chan Chen Hei.
- Singapore : Marshall Cavendish Cuisine, c2005.
p. cm.
ISBN : 981-261-009-X

1. Dim sum. 2. Cookery, Chinese. I. Title.

TX724.5.C5
641.5951 -- dc21   SLS2005002468

Printed in Singapore by Tien Wah Press (Pte) Ltd

contents

preface

When I think of dim sum, I think of the delicious street foods of China. Hot steaming *man tous* (buns) made on-the-spot, along with slippery smooth *ju cheong fun* (steamed rice rolls) doused with fragrant lard oil and large, juicy pork buns the size of Big Macs! Then there are grilled skewered squids dripping with peanut sauce and my personal favourite, grilled lamb fat. These dim sum may be coarsely made, but they are packed with taste and flavour!

The thought of dim sum also brings me back to my first year as an apprentice cook. Like other Cantonese chefs of my generation, I started my training in a dim sum kitchen. The restaurant I worked at was housed in a multi-storey building. The top floor was a lodging area for young apprentices like me and we shared it with pigeons, quails, chickens and ducks. As part of our training, we had to wake up at three every morning or be caned by the chefs. During business hours, we peddled dim sum from table to table. If we were slow in returning to the kitchen, we would be scolded. Whatever free time or energy we had left after work was spent conjuring up ways to appease the chefs. We would wash their dishcloths, buy them drinks or polish their battery of knives.

Although life as an apprentice cook was hard, I will always treasure the memories as it marks the start of my journey into the culinary world. It also introduced me to the art of dim sum making.

It may be easy to make dim sum, but to do it well is difficult. Even if you have mastered the techniques, the taste has to be perfected. I agree with the commonly held view that the earlier one picks up dim sum making, the better his or her skills will be. Young fingers are more nimble, making it is easier to fold 20 pleats on each dumpling. Young fingers are also more sensitive to the feel of the dough, an important requirement in gauging if the dough is of the correct texture or if it requires more kneading. The recipes in this book were chosen as they can be made by the home cook with some pastry know-how. All they need is practice and a little patience.

My first book, *The Art of Taste: Secrets of the Cantonese Kitchen* centres around what I do best — classic Cantonese cuisine. But for this second book, I want to share with readers what I have immense interest in — dim sum. Little tricks and techniques are given throughout this book to help you understand the art of dim sum making. I have also included some less common dim sum recipes which I hope will bring renewed interest in these once-popular morsels which have sadly been forgotten with time. Besides being a recipe resource, I hope this book will also serve as a modest documentary on dim sum.

Chef Chan Chen Hei

March 2005

"Today, the trend of making and presenting dim sum is continuing into two different but parallel directions — towards a modern, inventive and artful style; and a return to the traditional stalwart favourites. It is hard to say which one is better; it comes down to personal preference. Give me the simple, homey dim sum from the street stall anytime."

Chef Chan

Roast Pork and Preserved Mustard Cabbage Buns
Mui Choi Char Siew Bao 38

Steamed Pork Dumplings Topped with Crab Roe
Hai Wong Siew Mai 41

Crystal Duck Dumplings *Ye Ngap Choi Gau* 42

Steamed Radish Cake *Loh Bak Gou* 45

Soup Dumplings *Kun Tong Bao* 46

Steamed Fok Leng Pork Buns *Fok Leng Bao Zi* 49

White Jade Rolls with Crab Sauce
Hai Zap Bak Yok Qun 50

Sweet Potato Cake *Kam Xu Ma Lai Gou* 53

Steamed Custard Buns *Fong Wong Lau Sar Bao* 54

Sweet Bean Cake with Ginseng
Gao Lei Sum Mei Dao Gou 57

Sweet Black Sesame Rolls *Hak Zi Ma Qun* 58

Steamed Vegetable Dumplings *Zeng Fun Gor* 12

Phoenix Eye Prawn Dumplings
Fong Ngan Har Gau 15

Steamed Rice Rolls with Vegetables
Loh Hon Zai Cheong Fun 16

Steamed Pork Ribs and Black Olives on Rice Rolls
Larm Gok Pai Kuat Fun Qun 19

Four Treasures Wrapped with Chinese Yam
Wai San Sei Bao Zat 20

Twin Sausage Buns *Lap Cheong Qun* 23

Fragrant Curry Squid *Ka Li Heung Lat Sin Yao* 24

Stuffed Prawn Rolls *Sin Yok Har Tong* 27

Steamed Beef Balls *San Zok Ngao Yok* 28

Shark's Fin Dumplings with Bird's Nest Sauce
Yin Yek Yu Chee Gau 31

Chicken with Glutinous Rice *Lor Mai Gai* 32

Eel Dumplings *Seen Yok Gau* 37

steamed

MAKES 36

Ingredients

Cooking oil

Garlic — 3–4 cloves, peeled and chopped

Filling

Preserved radish (*choi bo*) — 70 g

Peanuts (groundnuts) — 70 g, roasted

Yellow chives (*gau wong*) — 70 g

Carrots — 70 g, peeled and diced

Yam bean (Chinese turnip) — 70 g, peeled and diced

Dried Chinese mushrooms — 30 g, soaked to soften, squeezed dry, stemmed and diced

Minced pork — 70 g

Superior stock (see pg 146) — 250 ml

Seasoning (to taste)

Oyster sauce

Dark soy sauce

Chinese *hua tiao* wine

Salt

Sugar

Ground white pepper

Dough

Wheat starch flour (*dung meen fun*) — 260 g

Corn flour (cornstarch) — 190 g

Water — 240 ml

Boiling water — 600 ml

Cooking oil — 75 ml

Steamed Vegetable Dumplings
Zeng Fun Gor 蒸粉果

When steamed, the skin of the dumplings becomes translucent, revealing the myriad of ingredients inside.

Method

- Heat some oil and sauté garlic until fragrant. Add filling ingredients except stock continue to sauté until fragrant.
- Add stock and seasoning to taste. Simmer until stock is slightly reduced and ingredients are cooked. Set aside to cool.
- Prepare dough. Combine wheat starch flour, 40 g corn flour and water to make a paste. Stir in boiling water and mix well. Add remaining corn flour and oil. Combine to form a dough.
- Roll dough out into a long cylinder. Cut into 36 equal pieces.
- Roll each dough piece out into a thin, round skin. Spoon some filling onto each skin and fold in half, forming a half moon. Pinch edges to seal.
- Arrange dumplings on an oiled steaming plate and steam over rapidly boiling water for 4 minutes.

MAKES 20

Ingredients

Pork (with some fat)	600 g, diced by hand
Prepared prawn (shrimp) meat*	200 g, diced by hand
Corn flour (cornstarch)	a pinch
Green peas	20

Seasoning (to taste)

Salt
Sugar
Ground white pepper
Sesame oil

Har gau dough

Wheat starch flour (dung meen fun)	65 g
Corn flour (cornstarch)	85 g
Hot water	150 ml

*Prepared prawn (shrimp) meat

- Peel and devein prawns. Measure amount of peeled prawns needed as specified in recipe.
- Place prawns in a colander and rub with a good amount of salt and corn flour. Rinse prawns with water while rubbing gently to remove skins. When salt and corn flour are fully rinsed out, transfer prawns to a bowl and immerse them in running water for 10 minutes. The prawns will take on a 'glassy' appearance and be crunchy when cooked.
- Drain well and use prawns according to recipe.

Phoenix Eye Prawn Dumplings
Fong Ngan Har Gau 凤眼虾饺

These prawn dumplings have a juicy, springy filling and translucent skin that is firm yet supple to the bite.

Method

- Scald pork briefly in boiling water. Drain well and allow to cool.
- Mix pork with prepared prawn meat and add seasoning to taste. Stir in corn flour to bind lightly. Set aside.
- Prepare *har gau* dough. Combine wheat starch flour and 20 g corn flour with hot water. Mix well. Add remaining corn flour and mix well until a smooth dough is achieved.
- Quickly roll dough into a cylinder and divide into 20 equal pieces. Roll each piece out into a thin, round skin. Use immediately.
- Place 1 heaped tsp of filling onto the centre of a dumpling skin. Fold in half, forming a half moon. Pinch both ends of the dumpling to seal, leaving the top exposed. Place a green pea on top. Repeat to make more dumplings. Arrange on an oiled steaming plate.
- Once dumplings are ready, steam immediately over rapidly boiling water for 3½–4 minutes. Maintain high heat throughout steaming. Serve immediately.

Note:
- Prepare the *har gau* skins as close to the cooking time as possible. Do not leave the prepared dough and skins aside for too long a time before using as they will not be translucent and supple when cooked.
- Roll out the skins as thinly as you can. Dim sum chefs use a cleaver specially made for flattening out dough into thin, round skins. You can find these cleavers at shops selling Chinese utensils (see pg 147).
- The secret to a juicy, springy filling is in pre-scalding the pork and dicing both the pork and prawns by hand.

MAKES 6

Ingredients

Cooking oil	
Carrots	115 g, peeled and julienned
Dried black fungus	20 g, soaked to soften, drained and julienned
Cabbage	40 g, julienned
Firm bean curd	115 g, julienned
Glass vermicelli (*fun xi*)	20 g, soaked to soften
Dried lily bulbs	20 g, soaked to soften and tough ends removed
Stock	3 Tbsp
Corn flour (cornstarch)	a pinch, mixed with some water

Seasoning (to taste)

Salt
Sugar
Sesame oil
Chinese *hua tiao* wine

Rice roll batter

Rice flour	60 g
Wheat starch flour (*dung meen fun*)	20 g
Salt	a pinch
Cooking oil	10 ml
Water	180 ml

Sauce

Superior stock (see pg 146)	60 ml
Light soy sauce	30 ml
Dark soy sauce	30 ml
Sugar	30 g
Sesame oil	to taste
Ground white pepper	to taste

Steamed Rice Rolls with Vegetables
Loh Hon Zai Cheong Fun 罗汉斋肠粉

Method

- Prepare sauce. Combine sauce ingredients and cook until slightly reduced and well blended. Set aside.

- Heat some oil and sauté carrots, black fungus, cabbage, bean curd, vermicelli and lily bulbs. Add stock and seasoning to taste. Thicken lightly with corn flour mixture. Set aside.

- Mix rice roll batter ingredients with sufficient water to form a paste that is not too thick or thin.

- Set a shallow, oiled tray or plate over rapidly boiling water.

- Pour a ladle of batter over tray or plate and spread evenly. When batter is almost cooked, spoon some filling on one side.

- Remove tray or plate from heat. Use a dough scraper to quickly and lightly roll up rice roll, starting at the side with filling. Place rice roll on a serving plate and continue to make more rice rolls until ingredients are used up.

- Spoon sauce over steaming hot rice rolls and serve immediately with lightly blanched vegetables as preferred.

Note: It takes experience to achieve a rice roll batter of the right consistency. The batter should be thin enough to allow the filling to show through the rice roll when steamed, and yet be thick enough to be rolled without breaking.

SERVES 12

Ingredients

Pork ribs (preferably whole prime ribs)	600 g, cut into 1-cm pieces
Salted black beans	50 g, crushed
Red chillies	1–2 , minced
Spring onions (scallions)	2–3, diced
Garlic	4 cloves, peeled and minced
Young ginger	50 g, peeled and minced
Corn flour (cornstarch)	a pinch
Rice roll batter (see pg 16)	½ recipe
Dried black olives (*larm gok*)	115 g, washed thoroughly to remove grit then blanched briefly, drained and rubbed with oil

Seasoning (to taste)

Light soy sauce

Dark soy sauce

Sugar

Ground white pepper

Sesame oil

Chinese *hua tiao* wine

Steamed Pork Ribs and Black Olives on Rice Rolls
Larm Gok Pai Kuat Fun Qun 橄角排骨粉卷

Method

- Marinate pork ribs with salted black beans, chillies, spring onions, garlic and young ginger. Add seasoning to taste. Add corn flour to bind lightly. Set aside.

- Make rice rolls as indicated in recipe for Steamed Rice Rolls with Vegetables (pg 16), without the vegetable filling.

- Cut rice rolls into bite-sized pieces and place on an oiled steaming plate. Spoon marinated pork ribs over and top with black olives.

- Steam over rapidly boiling water for 7–8 minutes. Serve immediately.

Note:

The purpose of cutting the steamed rice rolls into small, bite-sized pieces is to allow the rice rolls to better absorb the flavours from the pork ribs.

Do not add too much corn flour to the pork ribs as the dish should be fairly moist with sauce after steaming. Corn flour tends to dry up the dish.

MAKES 4

Ingredients

Chicken thigh	60 g, deboned and cut into strips
Chinese ham	35 g, cut into strips
Eel maw (see *Note*)	10 g
Dried Chinese mushrooms	5, soaked to soften, squeezed dry, stemmed and sliced
Corn flour (cornstarch)	a pinch
Chinese yam (*wai san*)	4 pieces, soaked in warm water to soften

Seasoning (to taste)

Salt

Sugar

Sesame oil

Chinese *hua tiao* wine

Sauce

Chicken stock	4 Tbsp
Oyster sauce	to taste
Dark soy sauce	to taste
Sesame oil	to taste
Salt	to taste
Sugar	to taste
Chinese *hua tiao* wine	to taste
Corn flour (cornstarch)	a pinch, mixed with some water

Four Treasures Wrapped with Chinese Yam

Wai San Sei Bao Zat 淮山四宝札

Method

- Combine chicken, ham, eel maw and mushrooms. Add seasoning to taste. Add corn flour to bind lightly then divide into 4 equal portions.

- Wrap each portion with a piece of Chinese yam. Place bundles on a steaming plate and steam over rapidly boiling water for 5–6 minutes.

- In the meantime, combine all sauce ingredients in a saucepan and cook until sauce is thickened.

- Pour sauce over steamed bundles and continue steaming for another 30 seconds before serving.

Note:

Soak the eel maw overnight to soften. You will notice that they have a rather fishy flavour. To remove the fishy smell, briefly boil the soaked eel maws in water mixed with some white vinegar. Rinse with cold water and repeat if necessary. Use eel maws according to the recipe.

Get the best quality of eel maw possible. It is less fishy.

When buying Chinese yam, ask for the thinner, longer pieces so they are easier to use as wrappers.

MAKES 18

Ingredients

Chinese sausages (*lap cheong*)	9
Chinese liver sausages (*ju gorn cheong*)	9

Bun dough

Low-gluten flour (*dai garn fun*)	600 g
Sugar	130 g
Baking powder	1 Tbsp
Instant dried yeast	1 tsp
Water	115 ml

Twin Sausage Buns
Lap Cheong Qun 腊肠卷

A great variety of dried and waxed meats can be found displayed outside restaurants in Hong Kong and Guangdong during the cold winter months.

These buns stuffed with dried sausages were once very popular, but they are now seldom found on dim sum menus, partly because diners are more health-conscious today. As a young child, I would just eat the sausages and leave the bun on the plate.

Method

- Steam sausages and cut each sausage lengthwise into half. Set aside.
- Combine all ingredients for bun dough and mix well to form a smooth dough. Leave to rest for 30 minutes.
- Roll dough out on a floured surface into a long cylinder. Divide into 18 equal pieces.
- Roll each dough piece into a long strip and coil it around a length each of sausage and liver sausage.
- Place buns on wax paper and steam over rapidly boiling water for 5 minutes.

SERVES 3–5

Ingredients

Fresh squid	300 g, cleaned and cut into bite-sized pieces
Curry powder	2 tsp
Chilli powder	1 tsp
Torch ginger bud	2 petals, minced
Young ginger	2-cm knob, peeled and minced
Garlic	3 cloves, peeled and minced
Leek	20 g, minced
Spring onions (scallions)	30 g, chopped
Minced bird's eye chilli	to taste
Chopped mint leaves	to taste (optional)
Coarsely ground green peppercorns	to taste (optional)
Corn flour (cornstarch)	a pinch

Seasoning (to taste)

Spicy bean paste

Salt

Sugar

Fragrant Curry Squid

Ka Li Heung Lat Sin Yao 咖喱香辣鲜鱿

Method

- Combine all ingredients and add seasoning to taste. Transfer to a steaming plate and steam immediately over rapidly boiling water for 3–4 minutes.

Note:

- The squid must be extremely fresh, not chilled overnight.
- Wash then cut squid, not vice versa, or the dish will be very watery when steamed.
- Do not over-steam squid. Even a few seconds can make a difference between a juicy, tender squid or one that is tough from being overcooked.

MAKES 12

Ingredients

Fresh large prawns (shrimps)	12, peeled
Pork (with some fat)	50 g, diced
Chinese celery	6 stalks, chopped
Spring onions (scallions)	3, chopped
Corn flour (cornstarch)	a pinch
Egg	1, beaten

Seasoning (to taste)

Salt

Ground white pepper

Sesame oil

Stuffed Prawn Rolls
Sin Yok Har Tong 鲜肉虾筒

Method

- Using a sharp knife, remove skin of prawns.
- Butterfly prawns. Cut down the back of each prawn from the head to the tail. Gently flatten prawns, slit side up, with the broad side of the knife. This will increase the surface area of the prawns for wrapping the ingredients.
- Scald pork in boiling water and pat dry. Mix with Chinese celery and spring onions. Add seasoning to taste. Bind lightly with corn flour.
- Divide pork mixture into 12 equal portions. Spoon a portion onto the middle of each prawn. Roll prawns up and seal with beaten egg.
- Arrange prawn rolls on an oiled steaming plate and steam over rapidly boiling water for 3–3^1/$_2$ minutes.
- Serve with a dip of your choice.

Note:
- After steaming, you can also pan-fry the prawn rolls and serve with a dip of garlic, chilli and white vinegar.
- As a variation to this recipe, use any other type of meat or filling as preferred.

MAKES 6

Ingredients

Beef	300 g, chopped by hand
Salt	1/2 tsp
Sugar	1/2 Tbsp
Bicarbonate of soda	1/4 tsp
Alkaline water (*garn soei*)	1/4 tsp
Water	150 ml
Cooking oil	
Dried bean curd skin (*fu pei*)	50 g
Watercress	a handful
Water chestnuts	40 g, peeled and finely chopped
Pork fat	40 g, chopped
Spring onions (scallions)	2, finely chopped
Chinese celery	1 stalk, finely chopped
Coriander (cilantro)	1 sprig, finely chopped
Dried orange peel	1 piece, finely chopped

Steamed Beef Balls
San Zok Ngao Yok 山竹牛肉

When steamed, the beef balls puff up. They are marvellously light, tender and springy.

Method

- Blend chopped beef in a food processor until pasty. Mix in salt, sugar, bicarbonate of soda, alkaline water and water. Refrigerate for 1 hour.
- Heat some oil and scald bean curd skin. Drain and soak in water until softened. Lay bean curd skin on a steaming plate. Set aside.
- Blanch watercress in lightly salted water. Drain and set aside.
- Add water chestnuts, pork fat, spring onions, Chinese celery, coriander and dried orange peel to chilled beef. Stir in 40 ml oil. Shape mixture into balls.
- Place watercress on bean curd skin and top with beef balls.
- Steam for 5–6 minutes. The beef balls will puff up. Serve with black vinegar or Worcestershire sauce.

Note: Use good quality bean curd skin, as it will not tear easily and thus be easier to handle.

MAKES 18

Ingredients

Filling

Ready-to-eat shark's fin	40 g
Prepared prawn (shrimp) meat (see pg 15)	80 g, diced by hand
Bamboo shoot	40 g, julienned
Chinese celery	2 stalks, chopped
Spring onions (scallions)	2, chopped
Corn flour (cornstarch)	a pinch

Seasoning (to taste)

Salt
Ground white pepper
Sesame oil

Bird's nest sauce

Bird's nest	12 g, soaked in warm water to soften
Superior stock (see pg 146)	110 ml
Salt	a pinch
Corn flour (cornstarch)	a pinch, mixed with some water
Har gau dough (see pg 15)	1 recipe

Shark's Fin Dumplings with Bird's Nest Sauce
Yin Yek Yu Chee Gau 燕液鱼翅饺

This is a luxurious treat temptingly wrapped in a delicate, translucent skin.

Method

- Combine filling ingredients except corn flour. Mix in seasoning to taste. Add corn flour to bind lightly. Set aside.
- Prepare bird's nest sauce. Cook bird's nest briefly in stock. Season with salt and thicken lightly with corn flour mixture. Remove from heat and allow to sit for 10 minutes.
- Prepare *har gau* dough as instructed on pg 15.
- Quickly roll dough into a cylinder and divide into 18 equal pieces. Roll each piece out into a thin, round skin (see *Note* on pg 15). Use immediately.
- Place 1 heaped tsp of filling on each skin. Fold in half, forming a half moon. Pinch both ends of dumpling, leaving rest of the top exposed. Add a few strands of shark's fin on top if desired.
- Arrange dumplings on an oiled steaming plate and steam over rapidly boiling water for $3^{1}/_{2}$–4 minutes, maintaining high heat throughout cooking.
- In the meantime, re-heat bird's nest sauce. Add a little more corn flour mixture to adjust sauce to your preferred thickness. Spoon sauce over dumplings to serve.

Note: As a variation to this recipe, you can add fresh scallop meat to the filling. You can also top the dumplings with crab roe, salmon roe or even caviar just before the end of steaming.

MAKES 5

Ingredients

Glutinous rice	600 g, washed, soaked overnight and drained
Dried lotus leaves	5

Filling

Chicken meat	150 g, sliced
Pork (with some fat)	35 g, sliced
Dried Chinese mushrooms	35 g, soaked to soften, squeezed dry, stemmed and sliced
Roasted pork (*char siew*)	35 g, sliced
Superior stock (see pg 146)	

Seasoning (to taste)

Salt

Sugar

Sesame oil

Dark soy sauce

Chicken with Glutinous Rice
Lor Mai Gai 糯米鸡

Method

- Cook glutinous rice in boiling water for 30 seconds. Drain and rinse to remove excess starch. Drain well.

- Spread rice over a steaming plate and steam for 15 minutes until partially cooked.

- Meanwhile, prepare filling. Place chicken, pork, mushrooms and roasted pork in a wok. Add enough stock to cover ingredients. Add seasoning to taste. Cook until filling is fairly moist with sauce but not too watery at the end of cooking.

- Place partially cooked glutinous rice in a bowl and add seasoning to taste.

- Divide glutinous rice into 5 parts. Place a portion onto a dried lotus leaf. Spread rice out over leaf and place cooked filling in the middle. Wrap up and secure with string. Repeat to make 4 more parcels.

- Steam parcels over high heat for 10 minutes. To serve, cut away a square of the leaf at the top of the parcel to show the cooked dish beneath.

Note:

When cooking the filling, pay close attention to the amount of sauce left at the end of cooking. This will affect the overall taste and flavour of the final dish. Too much sauce will cause the glutinous rice to become mushy and the filling will taste bland. Too little sauce and overall dish will be dry.

If the rice remains slightly hard after steaming, continue steaming for another 5–10 minutes.

MAKES 18

Ingredients

Har gau dough (see pg 15)	1 recipe

Filling

Eel	230 g, skinned, deboned thoroughly and diced by hand
Prepared prawn (shrimp) meat (see pg 15)	90 g, diced by hand
Pork	90 g, diced by hand
Preserved mustard cabbage (*harm choi*) stems	10 g, soaked (see *Note*) and diced
Ginger	2-cm knob, peeled and chopped
Spring onions (scallions)	2, chopped
Orange peel	1 piece, chopped
Corn flour (cornstarch)	a pinch

Seasoning (to taste)

Salt

Ground white pepper

Sesame oil

Sugar

Dark soy sauce

Eel Dumplings
Seen Yok Gau 鳝肉饺

When bitten into, the dumpling gives way to a warm, ginger-flavoured eel filling. The orange peel and salted vegetable help take the edge off the eel's assertive flavour.

Method

- Combine all filling ingredients except corn flour. Add seasoning to taste. Mix in corn flour to bind lightly.
- Prepare *har gau* dough as instructed on pg 15.
- Quickly roll dough into a cylinder and divide into 18 equal pieces. Roll each piece out into a thin, round skin (see *Note* on pg 15). Use immediately.
- Place 1 heaped tsp of filling on skin. Bring edge of skin up and pleat to seal dumpling. Repeat to make more dumplings.
- Arrange dumplings on an oiled steaming plate and steam immediately over rapidly boiling water for 5 minutes. Maintain high heat throughout cooking.
- Serve immediately with red vinegar or mustard. Both compliment the eel's strong flavour.

Note: Soak the preserved mustard cabbage in warm water for 5–10 minutes to get rid of any excess salt. Taste to check if it is still too salty. Soak for a while longer if necessary but do not leave it too long or the saltiness and flavour will be lost.

MAKES 18

Ingredients

Preserved mustard cabbage (*mui choi*)	300 g
Cooking oil	
Sugar	a pinch
Light soy sauce	
Superior stock (see pg 146)	450 ml + extra for steaming mustard cabbage
Roast pork (*char siew*)	300 g, diced
Spring onions (scallions)	4, chopped
Garlic	4 cloves, peeled and chopped
Young ginger	3-cm knob, peeled, smashed and chopped
Corn flour (cornstarch)	a pinch, mixed with some water

Seasoning (to taste)

Oyster sauce

Salt

Sugar

Char siew bao dough

Low-gluten flour (*dai garn fun*)	600 g
Sugar	130 g
Baking powder	1 Tbsp
Instant dried yeast	1 tsp
Water	115 ml

Roast Pork and Preserved Mustard Cabbage Buns
Mui Choi Char Siew Bao 梅菜叉烧包

Preserved mustard cabbage adds a fragrant, savoury depth to this classic dim sum.

Method

- Wash off excess salt and any grit in preserved mustard cabbage. Squeeze dry and shred finely. Fry in a little oil until fragrant. Steam with a pinch of sugar, some light soy sauce and enough stock to cover cabbage until softened. Remove from heat and drain.

- In a wok, add steamed preserved mustard cabbage, 450 ml stock, roast pork, spring onions, garlic, ginger and seasoning to taste. Cook for 2–3 minutes. Thicken with corn flour mixture. The resulting filling should be sweet, sticky and moist. Leave to cool.

- Combine all ingredients for the dough and mix well to form a smooth dough. Leave to rest for 30 minutes. Roll dough out on a floured surface into a long cylinder. Divide into 18 equal portions. Roll out each portion into a thin, round skin.

- Spoon some filling onto a dough skin. Bring edge of skin up and pleat to seal bun. Twist and pinch off any excess dough at the last pleat and place bun on wax paper, pleated side up. Repeat to make more buns.

- Steam buns over rapidly boiling water for 5 minutes.

Note:

▌ Exercise good judgment when thickening the filling with corn flour mixture. Adding too much will cause the filling to be dry when steamed and adding too little will cause the filling to taste flat and diluted.

▌ This recipe uses a yeast-based dough but there is another type of dough that uses starter dough (see pg 146). Buns made using starter dough are cottony in texture and will burst open when steamed.

MAKES 4

Ingredients

Ready-made *siew mai* skins	4 sheets
Fresh crab roe from 1 female crab	

Filling

Pork (preferably from hind leg)	70 g
Prepared prawn (shrimp) meat (see pg 15)	45 g
Corn flour (cornstarch)	a pinch

Seasoning (to taste)

Salt

Sugar

Ground white pepper

Sesame oil

Steamed Pork Dumplings Topped with Crab Roe

Hai Wong Siew Mai 蚧黄烧买

These Steamed Pork Dumplings (*Siew Mai*), together with Steamed Prawn Dumplings (*Har Gau*) and Roast Pork Buns (*Char Siew Bao*), are three of the most popular items at dim sum restaurants.

The secret to a juicy, springy dumpling is in the chopping of the filling. It should be done by hand so the meat is not too fine and retains its juiciness.

Method

- Prepare filling. Mince pork and prepared prawn meat using a cleaver. Add seasoning to taste then stir in corn flour to bind lightly.

- Divide mixture into 4 equal portions. Spoon a portion onto each *siew mai* skin. Press edges of skin together to hold filling in like a basket, leaving top exposed.

- Place dumplings on an oiled steaming plate. Cover and steam over rapidly boiling water for 3–4 minutes. Maintain high heat throughout cooking.

- Lift cover and spoon a small amount of crab roe on top of each dumpling. Replace cover and steam for another 30 seconds to 1 minute. Serve immediately.

Note:

- When increasing the serving size of this recipe, maintain the proportion of pork to prawns at 3:2.

- You can top the dumplings with roe before placing in the steamer, but this may cause the roe to become too dry.

- At some restaurants, salmon eggs are used in place of crab roe. I prefer crab roe for its inherent sweetness.

- You can make the dumplings in advance and refrigerate them. When needed, steam them for 4–5 minutes before topping with crab roe. Then steam for another 30 seconds to 1 minute and serve immediately.

MAKES 15

Ingredients

Duck meat	400 g, diced or cut into fine strips
Cooking oil	
Garlic	3–4 cloves, peeled and chopped
Ginger	3-cm knob, peeled and chopped
Spring onions (scallions)	75 g, chopped
Spinach	150 g, chopped
Bamboo shoot	75 g, chopped
Chinese celery	75 g, chopped
Superior stock (see pg 146)	300 ml
Corn flour (cornstarch)	a pinch, mixed with some water

Seasoning (to taste)

Salt
Light soy sauce
Sesame oil
Chinese *hua tiao* wine

Crystal skin dough

Corn flour (cornstarch)	100 g
Water	250 ml

Crystal Duck Dumplings
Ye Ngap Choi Gau 野鸭菜包

The translucent 'crystal' skin (*soei zeng pei*) of these dumplings allow the rich duck filling to show through, making them a treat for the eyes as well as the taste buds.

Method

* Mix duck meat with seasoning to taste.
* Heat some oil and sauté garlic, ginger and spring onions until fragrant. Add duck meat, spinach, bamboo shoot and Chinese celery. Mix well.
* Add stock and simmer over low heat until meat is cooked and stock is reduced slightly. Add corn flour mixture to thicken sauce lightly.
* Prepare crystal skin dough. Mix corn flour with 75 ml water into a paste. Boil remaining water and add to paste. Mix well to form a dough. Leave to rest for 10 minutes then knead dough until smooth. Roll out into a cylinder. Divide into 15 equal portions.
* Roll each dough piece out into a thin, round skin. Spoon some filling onto each skin and bring edge of skin up to enclose filling. Pinch edges to seal dumplings. Pinch off any excess dough. Repeat to make more dumplings.
* Arrange dumplings on an oiled steaming plate, pinched side down.
* Steam over rapidly boiling water for 3–4 minutes.

Note: The filling should be moist with some sauce but not too watery or thick. Keep watch over the heat level when cooking the filling and add the corn flour mixture judiciously.

MAKES A 45 X 45-CM CAKE

Ingredients

Cooking oil	
Dried prawns (shrimps)	190 g, diced
Dried Chinese sausages (*lap cheong*)	115 g, diced
Waxed pork (*lap yok*)	115 g, diced
Dried Chinese mushrooms	50 g, soaked to soften then squeezed dry and diced
Water	3 litres
Rice flour	600 g
Wheat starch flour (*dung meen fun*)	115 g
White radish	1.5–1.8 kg, peeled and grated

Seasoning (to taste)

Salt

Sugar

Sesame oil

Ground white pepper

Steamed Radish Cake
Loh Bak Gou 罗卜糕

Method

- Heat some oil and sauté dried prawns, sausages, waxed pork and mushrooms until fragrant. Add seasoning to taste.

- Stir in 2.5 litres water and bring to the boil.

- In the meantime, combine rice flour and wheat starch flour with remaining water to form a paste.

- Pour sautéed ingredients into paste and mix well. Transfer to a lightly oiled 45 x 45-cm tray.

- Steam over rapidly boiling water for 1 hour. Test for doneness by shaking tray gently. If the radish cake wobbles, steam for a while longer.

- Sprinkle your choice of garnish (chopped spring onion, fried shallots, red chilli slices) over cake just before removing from steamer.

- Cut into squares and serve. You can also pan-fry the radish cake squares lightly before serving.

MAKES 9

Ingredients

Filling

Prepared prawn (shrimp) meat (see pg 15)	550 g, chopped by hand
Pork	180 g, chopped by hand
Chinese parsley	3 sprigs, chopped
Spring onions (scallions)	3, chopped
Water	60 ml
Pig's skin aspic*	60 g, chopped

Seasoning

Sesame oil	to taste
Salt	to taste
Ground white pepper	to taste
Sugar	a pinch

Dough

High-gluten flour (*gou garn fun*)	230 g
Plain (all-purpose) flour	75 g
Water	140 ml
Cooking oil	20 ml

Soup Dumplings
Kun Tong Bao 灌汤包

This classic dumpling—literally a big dumpling pouch encasing a soupy stuffing—is becoming a rare find. Most dim sum restaurants serve it double-boiled in soup, instead of the traditional way, where the whole dumpling sits in a steaming basket. When well made, the dumpling skin is delicately thin yet strong enough to hold in its piping hot, soupy contents.

Method

- Combine filling ingredients. Add seasoning to taste.
- Mix dough ingredients to form a dough. Roll out onto a floured surface into a cylinder and divide into 9 equal portions.
- Roll out each dough piece into a thin, round skin. Spoon some filling onto each skin then fold into half, forming a half moon. Pleat edges to seal.
- Steam dumplings for 8–10 minutes until filling is cooked and pig's skin aspic melts.

*Pig's skin aspic

- Cut 120 g pig's skin into finger-width strips. Place in a shallow steaming bowl and fill with just enough water to immerse the strips. Place in a steamer and scatter over some chicken bones and strips of Chinese ham. Season with a pinch of salt. Steam for 2–3 hours until pig's skin dissolves. Strain and allow liquid to cool. When cooled, the liquid will jellify to become aspic. Use according to recipe. Refrigerate excess aspic for future use.

MAKES 18

Ingredients

Filling

Fok leng (poria cocos)	40 g
Water	115 ml
Pork (with some fat)	570 g, finely diced by hand
Chinese celery	70 g, finely diced by hand
Spring onions (scallions)	70 g, finely diced by hand
Corn flour (cornstarch)	a pinch

Seasoning (to taste)

Salt

Sugar

Sesame oil

Dough

Low-gluten flour (dai garn fun)	600 g
Sugar	130 g
Baking powder	1 Tbsp
Instant dried yeast	1 tsp
Water	115 ml

Steamed Fok Leng Pork Buns
Fok Leng Bao Zi 茯苓包子

The classic steamed pork bun is given a herbal twist with the addition of *fok leng* (poria cocos). This herb is good for the heart, spleen and lungs. It improves digestion and calms the mind.

Method

- Grind 20 g *fok leng* into a fine powder. You can ask the herbalist to grind it for you.
- Boil remaining *fok leng* with water. Discard *fok leng* and reserve liquid for dough.
- Combine pork, Chinese celery and spring onions with ground *fok leng*. Add seasoning to taste. Mix in corn flour to bind lightly.
- Combine dough ingredients and mix well to form a smooth dough. Leave to rest for 30 minutes.
- Roll dough out on a floured surface into a long cylinder. Divide into 18 equal pieces. Roll each dough piece out into a thin, round skin.
- Spoon some filling onto each dough skin and pleat edges to enclose filling. Twist and pinch off any excess dough at the last pleat. Place buns on wax paper, pleated side up.
- Steam buns over rapidly boiling water for 5 minutes.

Note: For the filling, use only light coloured seasoning and avoid dark coloured sauces to create a pristine look. If you prefer, you may add a little water to the filling so that it will be moist after steaming.

MAKES 10

Ingredients

Chinese cabbage (wong bok)	1

Filling

Prepared prawn (shrimp) meat (see pg 15)	90 g, diced by hand
Pork	90 g, diced by hand
Spring onions (scallions)	20 g, diced
Dried Chinese mushrooms	20 g, soaked to soften then squeezed dry and diced (optional)
Corn flour (cornstarch)	a pinch

Crab sauce

Crab meat	15 g
Crab roe from 1 female crab (optional)	
Superior stock (see pg 146)	4 Tbsp
Corn flour (cornstarch)	1 tsp, mixed with some water

Seasoning (to taste)

Salt

Sugar

Ground white pepper

Sesame oil

Chinese *hua tiao* wine

White Jade Rolls with Crab Sauce
Hai Zap Bak Yok Qun 蚧汁白玉卷

This classic dish inspires many variations. You can steam dainty portions in Chinese soup spoons for an elegant presentation or make larger bundles and serve them as a main dish. You can even omit the meat and turn this into a vegetarian treat.

Method

- Cut off both ends of cabbage. Discard any old, outer leaves and use only the tender, inner leaves. Blanch leaves briefly in boiling water then plunge into cold water. This will make the leaves crisp. Remove and drain well.

- Prepare filling. Combine prawn meat, pork, spring onions and mushrooms if using. Season with salt, sugar, pepper and sesame oil to taste. Mix in corn flour to bind lightly.

- Prepare crab sauce. Place crab meat, crab roe, if using, and stock in a saucepan and cook. Season to taste with salt, sesame oil and *hua tiao* wine. Stir in corn flour mixture to thicken. Set aside.

- Spoon some filling onto each cabbage leaf and roll up into a bundle. If leaves are too thick to be rolled, thin them down by slicing them horizontally. Instead of using large leaves, you can also overlap a couple of smaller leaves for the purpose.

- Place cabbage bundles, folded side down, on an oiled steaming plate and steam over rapidly boiling water for 4 minutes.

- Pour crab sauce over cabbage bundles and continue steaming for another 1 minute before serving.

Note: When making the crab sauce, ensure that it is sufficiently thick, as condensation during steaming may dilute it. The crab sauce should remain fairly thick at the end of steaming.

MAKES AN 18 X 18-CM CAKE

Ingredients

Starter dough (see pg 146)	300 g
Sugar	300 g
Eggs	6
High-gluten flour (*gou garn fun*)	20 g
Milk powder	230 g
Custard powder	230 g
Alkaline water (*garn soei*)	35 ml
Baking powder	1 tsp
Butter	115 g, melted
Sweet potatoes	300 g, peeled and grated

Sweet Potato Cake
Kam Xu Ma Lai Gou 甘薯马拉糕

This cake should rise well and have a close texture.

Method

- Combine starter dough, sugar, eggs, high-gluten flour, milk powder and custard powder and mix well. Leave aside for 12 hours.

- Add alkaline water, baking powder and butter and mix well. Add sweet potatoes and mix well.

- Pour mixture into a lined 18 x 18-cm baking tin. Steam over rapidly boiling water for 30 minutes. Slice to serve.

Note: For the best results, use a lined perforated tin when steaming the cake. This will enable the cake to rise beautifully.

MAKES 18

Ingredients

Salted egg yolks	5
Butter	75 g
Sugar	75 g
Condensed milk	5 Tbsp
Milk powder	20 g

Dough

Medium-gluten flour (*zong garn fun*)	600 g
Sugar	115 g
Cooking oil	40 ml
Instant dried yeast	1 tsp
Baking powder	1 tsp
Water	115 ml

Steamed Custard Buns
Fong Wong Lau Sar Bao 凤凰流沙包

Method

- Cream salted egg yolks, butter, sugar, condensed milk and milk powder together to form a paste. Set aside.
- Combine dough ingredients to form a smooth dough. Leave to rest for 1–2 hours until risen. Roll dough out on a floured surface into a long cylinder. Divide into 18 equal pieces.
- Roll each dough piece out into a thin, round skin. Spoon some salted egg mixture onto each skin. Bring edge of skin up to enclose filling. Pinch edges to seal buns. Place buns in patty tins, pinched side down.
- Steam over rapidly boiling water for 5 minutes.

MAKES A 28 X 28-CM CAKE

Ingredients

Black-eye beans (*mei dao*)	230 g
Water	
Water chestnut flour	190 g
Kingsford's corn flour (cornstarch) (*yin sok fun*)	75 g
Korean ginseng powder	a pinch
Agar-agar strips	12 g
Sugar	600 g

Sweet Bean Cake with Ginseng

Gao Lei Sum Mei Dao Gou 高丽参眉豆糕

Method

- Boil beans until soft and 90 per cent cooked. Drain and reserve liquid.
- Measure reserved liquid and top it up with more water to make up 2.4 litres. Return liquid to beans and add remaining ingredients. Cook until ingredients are well mixed.
- Transfer to a 28 x 28-cm baking tin and steam over rapidly boiling water for 30 minutes. Cut and serve warm or chilled.

Note: Kingsford's corn flour is a very high grade corn flour. This recipe will not work with other types of corn flour.

MAKES ABOUT 10

Ingredients

Black sesame seeds	120 g, roasted and finely ground
Sugar	180 g
Water chestnut flour	75 g
Water	360 ml

Sweet Black Sesame Rolls

Hak Zi Ma Qun 黑芝麻卷

Method

- Combine ingredients to form a batter.
- Set a shallow, oiled plate or tray over rapidly boiling water.
- Pour a ladle of batter on plate or tray and spread evenly. When batter sets, remove plate or tray from heat. Roll up tightly using a dough scraper. Continue to make more rolls until batter is used up. This recipe makes about 10 rolls, depending on the size of each roll.
- Chill sesame rolls before serving.

Note: The sesame rolls should have a springy feel. Rolling them up tightly after steaming will help.

fried

MAKES 30

Ingredients

Chinese chives (*gau choi*)	600 g, chopped by hand
Water chestnuts	190 g, peeled and diced
Pork (with some fat)	115 g, chopped by hand
Peeled prawns (shrimps)	115 g, chopped by hand
Corn flour (cornstarch)	a pinch
Cooking oil	

Seasoning (to taste)

Salt

Sugar

Ground white pepper

Sesame oil

Garlic oil

Dough

Plain (all-purpose) flour	450 g
High-gluten flour (*gou garn fun*)	150 g
Water	260 ml
Lard	40 g
Egg	1, beaten

Fried Chive Dumplings
Gau Choi Gok 韭菜角

Method

- Combine chives, water chestnuts, pork and prawns. Add seasoning to taste. Mix in corn flour to bind lightly. Set aside.

- Combine dough ingredients to form a dough. Leave to rest for 1 hour. Roll dough out on a floured surface into a long cylinder. Divide into 30 equal portions. Roll each portion out into a thin, round skin.

- Spoon some filling onto each skin and fold in half, forming a half moon. Pleat edges to seal or smear beaten egg around edges to seal.

- Heat oil and pan-fry dumplings over low heat. Serve with black vinegar and finely sliced young ginger strips.

Note: Getting the frying time right is crucial for this dish. Too long a time and the dumpling skin will blacken; too short and the filling will be uncooked. To make it easier, you can pre-steam the dumplings to ensure that the filling is cooked through before frying. This may, however, make the dumplings less fragrant.

MAKES 28

Ingredients

Beef	530 g, diced by hand
Chinese celery	150 g, chopped
Spring onions (scallions)	80 g, diced by hand
Corn flour (cornstarch)	a pinch
Cooking oil	

Seasoning (to taste)

Salt

Sesame oil

Dough

Water	270 ml
Plain (all-purpose) flour	460 g

Potsticker Dumplings
Wu Tip 锅贴

Method

- Combine beef with Chinese celery and spring onions. Add seasoning to taste. Add corn flour to bind lightly.

- Prepare dough. Heat half the water until hot. Add to half the flour and mix well. Mix remaining flour with remaining water (at room temperature) then combine both mixtures to form a dough.

- Roll dough out on a floured surface into a cylinder. Divide into 28 equal pieces then roll each piece out into a thin, round skin.

- Spoon some filling onto each skin. Fold one side of skin over filling then bring 2 opposite sides up and press together. The dumpling should be open at one end. Repeat to make more dumplings.

- Arrange dumplings on an oiled steaming plate. Steam over rapidly boiling water for 3–4 minutes.

- Heat some oil in a pan. Lay dumplings on pan to brown at the base.

- Serve with finely cut ginger strips and black vinegar.

MAKES 40

Ingredients

Filling

Carrots	120 g, peeled and julienned
White radish	120 g, peeled and julienned
Yam bean (Chinese turnip)	120 g, peeled and julienned
Peeled prawns (shrimps)	130 g, diced by hand
Mango flesh	130 g, cut into strips
Coriander (cilantro)	40 g, chopped
Spring onions (scallions)	40 g, chopped
Corn flour (cornstarch)	a pinch

Seasoning (to taste)

Salt

Sesame oil

Spring roll skins	40 sheets
Egg	1, beaten
Cooking oil for deep-frying	

Crispy Spring Rolls
Cui Pei Chun Qun 脆皮春卷

Method

- Combine filling ingredients except corn flour and season to taste. Add corn flour to bind lightly.

- On a flat working surface, position a spring roll skin with one corner pointing towards you. Spoon some filling on skin. Fold the left and right hand corners in over the fillng then fold the corner nearest you over them. Roll filling towards remaining corner to form a spring roll. Seal with beaten egg. Repeat to make more spring rolls.

- Heat oil for deep-frying. When oil is warm, gently lower spring rolls in. When spring rolls turn lightly golden, increase heat briefly. This reduces the absorption of oil into the rolls and also ensures that they are crispy. Remove and drain well.

- Serve spring rolls hot, with a dip made from plum sauce, chilli sauce and sugar.

Notes

Avoid cutting the mango too finely or it will turn to mush when deep-fried.

When deep-frying, keep the oil warm at around 50°C to enable the spring rolls to cook and brown evenly.

MAKES 4–6

Ingredients

Dried bean curd skin (*fu pei*)	1 sheet, cut into 4–6 pieces
Egg	1, beaten
Cooking oil	

Filling

Pork	90 g, diced
Peeled prawns (shrimps)	90 g, diced
Roast pork (*char siew*)	40 g, diced
Yellow chives (*gau wong*)	15 g, diced
Chinese chives (*gau choi*)	15 g, diced
Corn flour (cornstarch)	a pinch

Seasoning (to taste)

Salt
Sugar
Ground white pepper
Sesame oil

Crispy Bean Curd Skin Dumplings
Fu Pei Gok 腐皮角

Method

- Prepare filling. Mix pork, prawns, roast pork, yellow chives and chives with seasoning to taste. Mix in corn flour to bind lightly.
- Divide mixture into 4–6 equal portions. Place each portion on a piece of dried bean curd skin. Smear edge of dried bean curd skin with beaten egg and fold to enclose filling.
- Heat some oil and pan-fry dumplings over low heat until cooked and crisp. Drain well and serve with black vinegar or Worcestershire sauce.

Note: Pan-fry bean curd skin rolls on low heat to cook filling thoroughly. I prefer not to deep-fry the rolls as the bean curd skin will become too crisp and lose its delightful stretchy texture.

MAKES 12

Ingredients

Dough

Low-gluten flour (*dai garn fun*)	600 g
Starter dough (see pg 146)	115 g
Baking powder	½ Tbsp
Spring onion (scallion)	1, chopped
Red fermented bean curd (*nam yu*)	½ tsp
Five spice powder	a pinch
Salt	20 g
Water	230 ml

White sesame seeds
Cooking oil for deep-frying

Savoury Fried Bread
Harm Jeen Paeng 咸煎饼

Method

- Mix dough ingredients together to form a dough. Leave aside for 3 hours to rise.
- Roll dough out on a floured surface into a sheet 5-mm thick. Take one end of the dough and roll tightly towards the other end as with a Swiss roll.
- Cut into 12 equal portions. Lightly flatten each piece of dough cut-side up. Sprinkle with sesame seeds.
- Heat oil and deep-fry until brown and fragrant. Drain well before serving.

MAKES 25

Ingredients

Pork (with some fat)	350 g, diced by hand
Roast pork (*char siew*)	100 g, diced by hand
Dried Chinese mushrooms	6, soaked to soften, squeezed dry, stemmed and diced by hand
Superior stock (see pg 146)	350 ml
Corn flour (cornstarch)	a pinch, mixed with some water
Chinese chives (*gau choi*)	30 g, chopped
Cooking oil for deep-frying	

Seasoning

Dark soy sauce	to taste
Salt	to taste
Sugar	to taste
Five spice powder	a pinch
Sesame oil	to taste
Chinese *hua tiao* wine	to taste

Harm soei gok dough

Glutinous rice flour	600 g
Water	230 ml
Wheat starch flour (*dung meen fun*)	150 g
Hot water	150 ml
Sugar	150 g
Lard	225 g

Deep-fried Chewy Pork Dumplings
Harm Soei Gok 咸水角

These fried dumplings have a crisp and chewy skin and a savoury, moist pork filling.

Method

- Simmer pork, roast pork and mushrooms in superior stock. Add seasoning to taste and stir over low heat until ingredients are cooked.
- Stir in corn flour mixture to thicken slightly. Remove from heat and stir in chives. Allow to cool.
- Prepare dough. Mix glutinous rice flour with water and set aside. Mix wheat starch flour with hot water. Combine both mixtures, sugar and lard to make a dough.
- Divide dough into 25 equal parts. Roll each part out on a floured surface to get a thin, round skin.
- Spoon some filling onto each skin and fold into half, forming a half moon. Pinch edges to seal.
- Heat oil for deep-frying in a wok. Fry dumplings over low heat until firm. Turn up the heat slightly and continue to fry until dumplings are golden in colour. Just before removing dumplings, increase to high heat briefly. This reduces the absorption of oil into the dumplings and also ensures that they are crispy.

Note:

The sauce for the filling should not be too watery or thick. To achieve the right consistency, monitor the heat when cooking the filling and add the corn flour mixture judiciously.

Frying the dumplings over low heat in the beginning will prevent them from clumping together. Avoid stirring them in the oil at the start of deep-frying or they will stick to the cooking utensil. The dumplings should take 3–4 minutes to fry.

MAKES 28

Ingredients

Yam	600 g, peeled and sliced
Wheat starch flour (*dung meen fun*)	190 g
Lard	270 g

Filling

Chicken meat	370 g, diced by hand
Green peas	80 g
Onion	80 g, peeled and diced
Stock	260 ml

Seasoning (to taste)

Salt

Sugar

Ground white pepper

Sesame oil

Five spice powder

Cooking oil
for deep-frying

Crispy Yam Balls
Fong Chao Wu Gok 蜂巢芋角

Method

- Combine filling ingredients and cook until stock is reduced slightly. Add salt, sugar, pepper and sesame oil to taste. Allow to cool.

- Steam yam until soft then mash with flour and lard. Add seasoning to taste. Knead yam mixture until smooth, picking out any hard bits.

- Roll it out on a floured surface into long cylinder and divide into 28 equal pieces. Roll each piece out into a thin, round skin. Spoon some filling onto each piece and bring edges up to enclose.

- Heat oil for deep-frying and lower yam balls gently in, one at a time. Deep-fry until golden brown and drain well.

Note:

Keep the oil at about 70°C to deep-fry the dumplings. If the oil is too hot, the yam dumplings will turn dark and hard. A lower oil temperature will allow a lattice-like crust to form around the dumplings as they are being fried.

To fry several yam balls at a time, place them on a perforated metal tray. Ensure there is sufficient space between each ball for the crust to form, unobstructed. Gently immerse tray into warm oil to fry.

MAKES 15

Ingredients

Yam	800 g, peeled and shredded
Pork (with some fat)	150 g, minced
Salt	55 g
Sugar	55 g
Corn flour (cornstarch)	75 g
Five spice powder	a pinch
Sesame oil	a dash
Water	
Cooking oil	

Fried Shredded Yam
Wu Xi Paeng 芋丝饼

I personally prefer this version to the popular steamed yam and radish cakes. The shredded yam used here makes the dish more fragrant, especially after it is pan-fried.

Method

- Combine all ingredients except water and cooking oil. Mix well. Add a little water to bind mixture together.
- Spread mixture thinly over a square baking tin. Steam over rapidly boiling water for 25 minutes. Allow to cool before cutting into smaller pieces.
- Heat some oil and pan-fry steamed shredded yam pieces until crisp and fragrant.

MAKES 40

Ingredients

Black sesame seeds	60 g, roasted and ground
Green tea powder	20 g
Sugar	35 g
Butter	40 g
Cooking oil for deep-frying	

Glutinous rice dough

Glutinous rice flour	600 g
Wheat starch flour (*dung meen fun*)	115 g
Sugar	115 g
Lard	115 g
Green tea powder	1–2 Tbsp
Water	260 ml

Green Tea Glutinous Rice Balls
Lok Cha Tong Yun 绿茶汤丸

Method

- Cream ground black sesame seeds, green tea powder, sugar and butter together to form a paste. Set aside.
- Combine dough ingredients to form a soft dough. Roll it out into a long cylinder and cut into 40 equal pieces.
- Flatten each dough piece into a thin, round skin. Spoon some paste onto each skin and enclose filling. Roll into balls using both hands.
- Heat oil and deep-fry until light brown. Remove and drain well.

Note:
- The filling should be moist and runny when bitten into. When creaming the filling, check that the consistency is not too thick.
- The colour of green tea powder varies between different brands. As the glutinous rice dough should be very green, increase the amount of green tea powder used if necessary.

MAKES 30–40

Ingredients

Water chestnuts	200 g, peeled and diced
Water	1 litre
Custard powder	20 g
Sugar	380 g
Water chestnut flour	125 g
Cooking oil for deep-frying	

Batter

Plain (all-purpose) flour	300 g
Baking powder	1/2 Tbsp
Corn flour (cornstarch)	20 g
Water	
Cooking oil	100 ml

Water Chestnut Fritters
Zha Ma Tai Tiu 炸马蹄条

Method

- Cook water chestnuts with 500 ml water, custard powder and sugar. Stir until custard and sugar are dissolved.

- Mix water chestnut flour with remaining water. Add cooked water chestnut mixture and mix well.

- Transfer mixture to a 23 x 23-cm baking tin. Steam over rapidly boiling water for 25 minutes. Allow to cool and cut into 30–40 strips.

- Combine batter ingredients except oil, adding enough water so batter is of a thin consistency and pours in an even flow. Leave batter to rest for 30 minutes. Test the consistency again and add more water if necessary. Stir in oil and use batter immediately.

- Heat oil for deep-frying. Dip strips of water chestnut cake into batter and deep-fry until crisp. Remove and drain well.

Note: Do not dice the water chestnuts too finely or you would not be able to taste them. Do not cut them too coarsely either, or the dish will look rough.

MAKES 15

Ingredients

Potatoes	400 g, peeled, steamed and mashed
Glutinous rice flour	190 g
Sugar	260 g
Water	150 ml
Fine breadcrumbs	
Cooking oil for deep-frying	

Fried Potato Cakes
Xu Yong Paeng 薯茸饼

These fried potato cakes are golden and crisp outside and chewy inside.

Method

- Combine all ingredients except breadcrumbs and oil to form a dough. Add more water if mixture appears dry.
- Divide mixture into 15 equal portions. Shape each portion into a patty and coat with breadcrumbs.
- Heat oil to 80°C and deep-fry patties in batches. Cook each batch for about 3 minutes. Once patties puff up and float, they are cooked. Remove from oil and drain well before serving.

MAKES 25

Ingredients

Filling

Desiccated coconut	70 g
Sugared melon strips	45 g
Ground peanuts (groundnuts)	45 g
White sesame seeds	35 g + extra for coating
Sugar	35 g

Chewy pumpkin dough

Pumpkin flesh	150 g, steamed and mashed
Glutinous rice flour	150 g
Wheat starch flour (*dung meen fun*)	55 g
Sugar	75 g

Water

Cooking oil

Fried Chewy Pumpkin Cakes
Lam Gua Paeng 南瓜饼

Method

- Combine filling ingredients and set aside.
- Combine dough ingredients with enough water to form a pliable dough. Roll it out on a floured surface into a cylinder. Divide into 25 equal portions.
- Roll each portion out into a thin, round skin. Spoon some filling onto each skin and enclose. Flatten cakes lightly.
- Arrange on an oiled steaming plate and steam over rapidly boiling water for 3 minutes. Allow to cool.
- Sprinkle some sesame seeds over steamed cakes. Heat some oil and pan-fry cakes until lightly crisp before serving.

MAKES 15

Ingredients

Dough

Glutinous rice flour	300 g
Sugar	115 g
Baking soda	1/2 tsp
Cooking oil	20 ml
Water	150 ml
White sesame seeds	2 Tbsp

Cooking oil
  for deep-frying

Hollow Fried Balls
Hong Sum Jeen Tui 空心煎堆

When deep-fried, the dough puffs up with a crispy, wafer-thin crust. In the past, the balls were filled with a mix of ground peanuts, olive seeds (*larm yarn*), almonds and sugar. Perhaps these were too rich, as they are now less popular. The hollow version, however, remains a firm favourite at some Hong Kong eateries.

When I was growing up in Shun Tak, my parents used to make the filled ones on the eve of the Lunar New Year. Any leftovers would be stored in the rice urn—the wintry weather preserved them well and we were able to enjoy them over the following weeks!

Method

- Combine all dough ingredients except sesame seeds to form a dough.
- Divide dough into 15 equal pieces. Roll each piece into a ball and coat with sesame seeds.
- Heat oil over medium heat and gently place balls in. Push them down with the back of spatula or strainer and then release to allow the balls to rise and expand. Repeat a few more times until the balls balloon and turn golden brown.
- Remove and drain well before serving.

Note: When deep-frying, keep a close watch over the heat level as the dough burns easily.

MAKES 12

Ingredients

First dough (soei pei)

Medium-gluten flour (*zong garn fun*)	600 g
Starter dough (see pg 146)	115 g
Sugar	75 g
Lard	40 g
Baking powder	1/2 Tbsp
Egg	1
Water	190 ml

Second dough (yao sum)

Low-gluten flour (*dai garn fun*)	300 g
Sugar	115 g
Lard	20 g
Water	75 ml

Cooking oil for deep-frying

Beef Tongue Bread
Ngao Lei Soh 牛脷酥

Nicknamed "*ngao lei*", meaning "beef tongue" because of its shape, this sweet, fried bread with a crunchy top is a popular breakfast item in Hong Kong. It is made by combining two types of dough—a lighter "*soei pei*" (water skin) and a sugary and heavier "*yao sum*" (oily centre). When deep-fried, the latter caramelises and forms swirls in the fluffy bread.

Method

- Mix first dough ingredients to form a dough. Leave to rise for 3 hours.
- Mix second dough ingredients to form a dough.
- Roll first dough out on a floured surface until it is large enough to enclose second dough. Bring sides of first dough up to enclose second dough. Roll out combined dough. Fold in the sides and roll out again. Repeat the folding and rolling out of dough a few more times.
- Roll dough out into a 5-mm thick sheet. Take one end of the dough and roll tightly towards the other end as you would a Swiss roll. Cut into 12 equal portions. Lightly flatten each piece of dough, cut-side up.
- Heat oil and deep-fry dough pieces until brown. Remove and drain well before serving.

MAKES ABOUT 30

Ingredients

Lard	15 g
Water	380 ml
Plain (all-purpose) flour	300 g
Eggs	8
Cooking oil for deep-frying	
Confectioners' (icing) sugar	

Fried Egg Puffs
Zha Dan Kao 炸旦球

Method

- Cook lard, adding a little water at a time until lard is dissolved. Bring to a gentle boil.
- Pour lard mixture into flour and mix well. Add in eggs, one at a time, mixing well after each addition.
- Heat oil for deep-frying. While egg mixture is still warm, use a Chinese soup spoon to scoop up a ball of the mixture. Slide mixture into oil and deep-fry until puffed up. Remove and drain well. Continue frying until egg mixture is used up.
- Dust confectioners' sugar over warm egg puffs and serve.

Note: When deep-frying, maintain the oil temperature at 70–80°C. If the heat is too high, the puffs will brown on the outside without cooking on the inside. The puffs should be crisp outside and light and fluffy inside.

MAKES 30

Ingredients

Cooking oil	
Beef	600 g, diced by hand
Green peas	60 g
Potatoes	60 g, peeled and diced
Green chillies	25 g, minced
Spring onions (scallions)	25 g, chopped
Young ginger	25 g, peeled and chopped
Stock	3–5 Tbsp
Corn flour (cornstarch)	a pinch, mixed with some water

Seasoning (to taste)

Curry powder
Salt
Sugar
Chinese *hua tiao* wine
Sesame oil

First dough (soei pei)

Medium-gluten flour (*zong garn fun*)	600 g
High-gluten flour (*gou garn fun*)	75 g
Sugar	75 g
Eggs	2, beaten
Water	230 ml

Second dough (yao sum)

Low-gluten flour (*dai garn fun*)	600 g
Lard	380 g

Flaky Beef Puffs
Ngao Yok Soh 牛肉酥角

Method

* Heat some oil and sauté beef, green peas, potatoes, green chillies, spring onions and young ginger until fragrant. Add stock and seasoning to taste. Mix well then add corn flour mixture to bind lightly. Allow to cool.

* Combine first dough ingredients to form a dough.

* Combine second dough ingredients to form a dough.

* Roll first dough out on a floured surface until it is large enough to enclose second dough. Place second dough in the middle of first dough and enclose. Roll combined dough out and fold in the sides then roll out again. Repeat the process of folding and rolling a few more times. Leave dough in the refrigerator for 1 hour.

* Roll chilled dough out on floured surface. Fold it in half and roll up tightly from the shorter end as you would a Swiss roll. Cut into 30 equal rounds. Flatten each round out.

* Spoon some beef filling onto each round and fold in half, forming a half moon. You should be able to see the layers of dough on the outside of the puffs. Pinch edges to seal.

* Heat enough oil for deep-frying. Fry puffs for about 6 minutes over fairly low heat. When puffs are golden brown, increase heat briefly. This reduces the absorption of oil into the puffs and also ensures that they are crispy. Remove and drain well.

Note:

▮ For these puffs to taste good, ensure that the filling is fairly moist after sautéing. Add more stock if necessary.

▮ When deep-frying the puffs, the oil should not be too hot. Turn off the heat mid-way through frying if necessary.

▮ Increase the temperature of the oil to about 80°C at the last moments of cooking by spooning away some oil from the wok.

Flaky Vegetable Puffs
Choi Xi Soh 菜丝酥

Ingredients

Cooking oil	
White radish	450 g, peeled and shredded
Cabbage	130 g, shredded
Dried black fungus	50 g, soaked to soften and shredded
Minced pork	80 g
Spring onions (scallions)	50 g, shredded
Young ginger	50 g, peeled and shredded
Dried prawns (shrimps)	50 g, soaked and chopped

Seasoning (to taste)

Salt	
Sesame oil	

First dough (soei pei)

Medium-gluten flour (zong garn fun)	300 g
Sugar	40 g
Egg	1, beaten
Lard	40 g
Water	115 ml

Second dough (yao sum)

Low-gluten flour (dai garn fun)	300 g
Lard	1

Method

- Heat some oil and sauté radish, cabbage, black fungus, minced pork, spring onions, ginger and dried prawns until fragrant. Add seasoning to taste. Set aside to cool.
- Combine first dough ingredients to form a dough.
- Combine second dough ingredients to form a dough.
- Roll first dough out on a floured surface until it is large enough to enclose second dough. Place second dough in the middle of first dough and bring sides up to enclose. Roll combined dough out and fold in the sides then roll out again. Repeat the process of folding and rolling out the dough a few more times. Leave dough in the refrigerator for 1 hour.
- Roll chilled dough out on a floured surface. Fold dough in half and roll up tightly from the shorter end as with a Swiss roll. Cut into 12 equal slices then halve each slice horizontally to get 2 semi-circular pieces.
- Stand each semi-circle on its freshly-cut side. Using your palm, press each semi-circle down to flatten then roll each one out into a long strip.
- Spoon some filling on top, nearer one end of dough strip and roll dough up like a Swiss roll to enclose filling. You should be able to see the layers of dough on the outside of the puff. Repeat to make more puffs.
- Heat oil for deep-frying. Fry puffs for 3–4 minutes over low heat. When puffs are golden brown, increase heat briefly. This reduces the absorption of oil into the puffs and also ensures that they are crispy. Remove and drain well.

Note: The proportion of flaky crust should be more than the filling, so try not to put too much filling into each puff.

MAKES 1 LARGE PANCAKE

Ingredients

Red bean paste	75 g
Cooking oil	
Pine nuts	10, toasted

Batter

Plain (all-purpose) flour	60 g
Corn flour (cornstarch)	10 g
Custard powder	10 g
Egg	1, beaten
Water	150 ml

Red Bean Pine Nut Pancake
Song Chee Wu Paeng 松子窝饼

Method

- Combine batter ingredients and set aside.
- Spread red bean paste into a square between 2 layers of plastic wrap.
- Heat a wok and grease lightly with some oil. Pour batter into wok and tilt wok around so batter coats wok evenly. Cook over low-medium heat until partially set.
- Holding red bean paste square in one hand, remove the top sheet of plastic wrap with the other hand. Flip red bean paste onto the centre of pancake in wok. Peel away the other piece of plastic wrap. Sprinkle pine nuts over.
- Use a spatula to fold in the sides of pancake to cover red bean paste. Flip pancake over to fry other side until crisp. Increase heat if necessary.
- Remove from heat. Cut pancake into 2 rectangular halves then cut into bite-sized pieces.

MAKES 25

Ingredients

Red bean paste	380 g
Harm soei gok dough (see pg 73)	1 recipe
White sesame seeds	
Cooking oil	

Fried Chewy Red Bean Cakes
Lor Mai Paeng 糯米饼

Method

- Divide red bean paste into 25 equal portions.
- Prepare *harm soei gok* dough as instructed on pg 73. Roll it out on a floured surface into a long cylinder. Divide into 25 equal pieces.
- Roll each dough piece out into a thin, round skin. Place a portion of red bean paste on each skin and enclose.
- Press to flatten cake slightly then coat with sesame seeds. Arrange on an oiled steaming plate and steam over rapidly boiling water for 3–4 minutes.
- Heat a pan and coat with some oil. Pan-fry steamed cakes until fragrant and golden brown.

baked

MAKES 30–35

Ingredients

Lotus seed paste	200 g
Century eggs	8–9, peeled, washed and cut into quarters
Red ginger slices	30–35
Egg	1, beaten
White sesame seeds	

First dough (soei pei)

Medium-gluten flour (*zong garn fun*)	600 g
Cooking oil	75 ml
Sugar	75 g
Egg	1
Water	190 ml

Second dough (yao sum)

Low-gluten flour (*dai garn fun*)	600 g
Lard	225 g

Flaky Century Egg Pastries
Pei Dan Soh 皮旦酥

These gold nugget-shaped pastries were once presented as gifts during Chinese weddings. The pastry crust is similar to that of Wife Cakes (*Loh Por Paeng*) on pg 107.

Method

- Combine first dough ingredients to form a dough.
- Combine second dough ingredients to form a dough.
- Roll first dough out on a floured surface until it is large enough to enclose second dough. Place second dough in the middle of first dough and bring sides up to enclose. Roll out combined dough and fold in the sides of the dough. Repeat the process of rolling and folding a few more times. Leave dough in the refrigerator for 1 hour.
- Roll chilled dough out into a long cylinder and divide into 30–35 equal pieces. Roll each dough piece out into a thin, round skin.
- Place some lotus seed paste, a century egg quarter and a red ginger slice onto each skin and enclose. Press gently to form a nugget. Arrange on a baking tray.
- Brush nuggets with beaten egg and sprinkle sesame seeds over.
- Bake in a preheated oven at 200°C for 8 minutes.

MAKES 35

Ingredients

Eggs	1, beaten
White sesame seeds	

Filling

Fried rice flour (*gou fun*)	600 g
Sugar	600 g
Olive oil	75 ml
Desiccated coconut	150 g
Sugared winter melon strips	300 g, chopped
Peanuts (groundnuts)	115 g, roasted and ground
Olive seeds (*larm yarn*)	150 g, roasted and coarsely ground
Water	600 ml

First dough (*soei pei*)

Medium-gluten flour (*zong garn fun*)	600 g
Cooking oil	75 ml
Sugar	75 g
Egg	1
Water	190 ml

Second dough (*yao sum*)

Low-gluten flour (*dai garn fun*)	600 g
Lard	225 g

Wife Cakes
Loh Por Paeng 老婆饼

The filling for these pastries used to be rich with lard, but today, olive oil and sugared melon strips are used instead.

Method

- Combine filling ingredients to form a paste. Set aside.
- Mix first dough ingredients to form a dough.
- Mix second dough ingredients to form a dough.
- Roll first dough out on a floured surface until it is large enough to enclose second dough. Place second dough in the middle of first dough and bring up the sides to enclose. Roll out combined dough and fold in the sides then roll out again. Repeat the process of folding and rolling out the dough a few more times. Leave dough in the refrigerator for 1 hour.
- Roll dough out into a long cylinder and divide into 35 equal pieces. Roll each dough piece into a thin, round skin. Spoon some filling onto each skin and enclose.
- Flatten pastry slightly and arrange on a baking tray. Brush with beaten egg and sprinkle with sesame seeds.
- Bake in a preheated oven at 200°C for 8 minutes.

MAKES 30

Ingredients

White lotus seed paste	125 g
Salted egg yolks	15, each cut in half
Egg	1, beaten
White sesame seeds	

Flaky puff dough

Medium-gluten flour (*zong garn fun*)	300 g
Cooking oil	40 ml
Sugar	40 g
Water	115 ml

Flaky Lotus Seed Paste and Salted Egg Yolk Pastries
Wong Kam Soh 黄金酥

Method

- Prepare flaky puff dough. Mix dough ingredients together to form a dough.

- Roll dough out on a floured surface to 2-mm thick. Use a 6-cm round cutter to cut out 30 rounds.

- Divide lotus seed paste into 30 equal portions.

- Place a portion of lotus seed paste and a salted egg yolk half onto each dough circle and enclose filling.

- Arrange on a baking tray. Brush with beaten egg and sprinkle with sesame seeds.

- Bake in a preheated oven at 200°C for 7–8 minutes.

MAKES 30

Ingredients

Pork (with some fat)	115 g
Sugar	
Chinese rose wine	a dash
Ground peanuts (groundnuts)	150 g
Ground white sesame seeds	150 g
Flaky puff dough (see pg 108)	1 recipe
Egg	1, beaten
White sesame seeds	

Sugared Pork Puffs
Peng Yok Soh 冰肉酥

Method

- Blanch pork in boiling water until partially cooked. Remove, drain and pat dry. Chop finely by hand.

- Spread sugar and rose wine over pork. Use enough sugar to cover pork. Leave to marinate in the refrigerator for 1 week. The pork will crystallise (see *Note*). Rinse in water to remove excess sugar then pat-dry before using.

- Mix crystallised pork with ground peanuts and sesame seeds. Set aside.

- Prepare flaky puff dough as instructed on pg 108. Divide dough into 2 equal portions. Roll each portion out on a floured surface into a rectangular sheet, 10-cm wide and 2-mm thick.

- Spread filling onto 1 sheet of dough then sandwich with other sheet of dough. Press edges to seal and place on a greased baking tray. Without cutting through the pastry, make shallow cuts across width of pastry to get 30 equal puffs.

- Brush with beaten egg and bake in a preheated oven at 220°C for 6–8 minutes. Sprinkle sesame seeds over towards the end of baking.

- Cut to serve.

Note: After the pork has been marinated for 1 week, it should be hard and crisp to the touch. If it does not feel firm, it means that not enough sugar was used. Discard and make a new batch before proceeding with the rest of the recipe.

MAKES 25

Ingredients

Filling

Desiccated coconut	150 g
Sugar	270 g
Egg	1, beaten
Olive oil	40 ml
Milk powder	20 g
Water	

First dough (soei pei)

Medium-gluten flour (*zong garn fan*)	300 g
Cooking oil	40 ml
Sugar	40 g
Egg	1, beaten
Water	115 ml

Second dough (yao sum)

Low-gluten flour (*dai garn fan*)	300 g
Butter	60 g
Lard	600 g

Coconut Tarts

Ye Tat 椰挞

Like Ginger Egg Tarts (*Keong Zap Dan Tat*) on pg 116, the crust for these tarts is made using two types of dough to create a flaky pastry. The first dough is a water-based dough called "*soei pei*" (water skin) while the second dough is a rich oil-based dough called "*yao sum*" (oily centre).

Method

- Combine and cream filling ingredients adding a little water at a time until a paste is formed. Set aside.
- Combine first dough ingredients to form a dough.
- Combine second dough ingredients to form a dough.
- Roll first dough out on a floured surface until it is large enough to enclose second dough. Place second dough in the middle of first dough and bring the sides up to enclose. Roll out combined dough on a lightly floured surface and fold in the sides then roll out again. Repeat the process of folding and rolling out the dough a few more times. Refrigerate dough for 1 hour.
- Roll dough out into a 2-mm thick sheet. Use a 6-cm round cutter to cut out rounds from dough. Grease tart cases and press in dough circles.
- Fill tart cases with prepared filling. Bake in a preheated oven at 200°C for 6–8 minutes.

Note:
To remove the baked tarts from the tart cases, give the cases a gentle shake. The tarts will be dislodged.

Flaky Haw Pastries
San Zha Soh Paeng 山楂酥饼

MAKES 30–35

Ingredients

Filling

Haw flakes (*san zha*)	680 g, crushed
Chinese yam powder (*wai shan fun*)	130 g
Pine nuts	50 g, ground
Water	
Sugar	to taste
First and second dough from Wife Cakes (see pg 107)	1 recipe each
Eggs	2, beaten
White sesame seeds	

This dim sum has a rich, flaky crust and a thin layer of sweet-sour haw filling. Chinese yam makes this tasty treat good for digestion too.

Method

- Prepare filling. Combine haw flakes, Chinese yam powder and ground pine nuts. Add just enough water to cover ingredients then mix well to form a paste. Add sugar to taste.
- Prepare first and second dough then combine as instructed on pg 107.
- Roll dough out on a floured surface into a long cylinder. Divide it into 30–35 equal pieces. Roll each dough piece out into a thin, round skin. Spoon some filling onto each skin and enclose.
- Flatten pastry slightly and arrange on a baking tray. Brush with egg and sprinkle with sesame seeds.
- Bake in a preheated oven at 200°C for 8 minutes.

Note:

Chinese yam powder is available from Chinese herbal shops. Ask for "*wai shan fun*".

The proportion of crust should be greater than the filling, so avoid spooning too much filling onto the dough when making the pastries.

MAKES 25

Ingredients

Eggs	4
Water	300 ml
Sugar	to taste
Ginger juice (see *Note*)	to taste
First and second dough from Coconut Tarts (see pg 112)	1 recipe each

Ginger Egg Tarts
Keong Zap Dan Tat 姜汁旦挞

Method

- Prepare first and second dough then combine as instructed on pg 112.
- Roll dough out into a 2-mm thick sheet. Use a 6-cm round cutter to cut out rounds from dough. Grease tart cases and press in dough circles.
- Beat eggs with water, sugar and ginger juice. Strain mixture into a jug or teapot and pour into prepared tart cases.
- Bake in a preheated oven at 250°C for 8–10 minutes.

Note:

To obtain ginger juice, finely grate a knob of fresh ginger. Squeeze the pulp for juice then discard the pulp.

To avoid overcooking custard, remove tarts from oven when custard is still moist to the touch. Cover tarts to allow residual heat to cook the custard further. In this way, the custard will be cooked yet soft.

MAKES 20

Sugar-crusted Buns with Fresh Pineapple Filling
Po Loh Bao 菠萝包

A popular breakfast and teatime treat in **Hong Kong**, this bun is filled with fresh pineapple and capped with a flaky, sugary crust.

MAKES 20

Ingredients

Filling

Fresh, skinned pineapple	450 g, diced
Sugar	to taste
Water	
Custard powder	1 Tbsp
Custard cream	50 g

Basic dough

High-gluten flour (*gou garn fun*)	300 g
Egg	1, beaten
Instant dried yeast	1/4 tsp
Sugar	40 g
Butter	20 g
Water	

Sugary puff dough

Low-gluten flour (*dai garn fun*)	300 g
Sugar	115 g
Egg	1, beaten
Baking powder	1/4 tsp
Ammonia powder (*chow fun*)	1/4 tsp
Butter	25 g

Method

- Prepare filling. Cook pineapple with sugar and in enough water to immerse it. Cook until a jam-like consistency is reached.
- Add custard powder and custard cream and cook until well-blended. Remove from heat and allow to cool.
- Combine basic dough ingredients and mix well with enough water to form a pliable dough. Leave to rest for 30 minutes. Roll dough out into a long cylinder and divide into 20 equal pieces.
- Combine sugary puff dough ingredients and mix well to form a dough. Roll dough out into a sheet and cut into 20 squares.
- Roll a piece of basic dough out into a thin skin and spoon some pineapple filling onto it. Pleat edges to enclose filling. Twist and pinch off any excess dough at the last pleat and place bun on a baking tray, pleated side up. Top bun with a square of sugary puff dough. Repeat to make more buns.
- Bake buns in a preheated oven at 200°C for 8–10 minutes.

MAKES 30 BOWLS

Ingredients

Dried vegetables (*choi gorn*)	115 g
Pork bone (preferably whole leg bone)	400 g
Rice	500 g, washed and drained
Glutinous rice	150 g, washed and drained
Water	7–9 litres
Dried orange peel	3–4 pieces
Ginger slices	5–7, each about 1-cm thick

Dried Vegetable Congee
Choi Gorn Chok 菜干粥

Back in my hometown of Shun Tak, Canton, the womenfolk would dry the cabbage in the sun and store it for use in soups and congees like this dish. Whole pork bone gives this humble dish a strong, meaty fragrance.

Method

- Wash dried vegetables thoroughly then soak for 1–2 hours to remove excess salt. Rinse well and chop into small pieces.
- Combine all ingredients in a pot and simmer for 2–3 hours. Serve hot.

MAKES 20

Ingredients

Filling

Water chestnuts	90 g, peeled and finely diced
Chinese chives (*gau choi*)	90 g, finely chopped
Spring onions (scallions)	90 g, finely chopped
Coriander (cilantro)	90 g, finely chopped
Corn flour (cornstarch)	a pinch

Seasoning (to taste)

Salt
Ground white pepper
Sesame oil

Fish dough

Mud carp (*lei yu*) fillet	400 g, skinned and deboned
Low-gluten flour (*dai garn fun*)	600 g
Cooking oil	75 ml
Water	230 ml

Fish Dumplings
Yu Pei Gau 鱼皮饺

These dumplings have a skin made from the sweet flesh of mud carp, and a filling of crunchy vegetables.

Method

- Combine all filling ingredients except corn flour. Add seasoning to taste. Mix in corn flour to bind lightly.
- Dice fish meat by hand then mash. Mix with flour, oil and water to form a dough. Knead until dough is very smooth.
- Roll dough out on a floured surface into a cylinder. Divide into 20 equal pieces. Roll dough pieces out into thin, round skins.
- Spoon some filling onto each skin and fold in half, forming a half moon. Cup dumpling with both hands then use both thumbs to squeeze dumpling gently to seal edges. Repeat to make more dumplings.
- Cook dumplings in gently boiling water and drain well.
- Serve with sliced chillies in light soy sauce, vinegar or mustard sauce.

Note: As an alternative, you can pan-fry the dumplings lightly before serving, or serve them with noodles in soup.

MAKES 35

Ingredients

Ready-made *wan tan* skins	35 sheets
Stock	1.2 litres
Spring onion (scallion)	1, chopped

Filling

Fresh lean pork	340 g, diced by hand
Peeled prawns (shrimps)	140 g, diced by hand
Dried black fungus	20 g, soaked to soften, drained and shredded
Ginger	40 g, peeled and shredded
Spring onions (scallions)	40 g, shredded
Chinese chives (*gau choi*)	40 g, shredded
Chinese celery	40 g, shredded

Seasoning (to taste)

Salt

Sesame oil

Ground white pepper

Fresh Pork Dumplings
Ju Yok Wan Tan 猪肉云吞

Method

- Combine filling ingredients and add seasoning to taste.
- Spoon some filling onto a *wan tan* skin and enclose. Repeat to make more dumplings.
- Cook dumplings in boiling water for 3 minutes then drain well.
- Add to stock and bring to the boil for 2 minutes to further remove any alkaline taste from *wan tan* skins.
- Serve hot, sprinkled with chopped spring onions.

Note: Instead of serving these dumplings in soup, blanch then drain them and serve with a spicy dip of dark soy sauce, sugar, salt, Chinese *hua tiao* wine, sesame oil, chopped spring onions, chopped Chinese celery and Sichuan chilli paste.

MAKES 24

Ingredients

Superior stock (see pg 146)	1.4 litres
Yellow chives (*gau wong*)	4–5 stalks, sliced

Filling

Peeled prawns (shrimps)	180 g, chopped by hand
Pork	300 g, chopped by hand
Chinese celery	20 g, chopped
Spring onions (scallions)	20 g, chopped
Dried Chinese mushrooms	10 g, soaked to soften, squeezed dry, stemmed and finely chopped
Dried black fungus	10 g, soaked to soften, drained and finely chopped
Carrots	20 g, peeled and finely chopped
Bamboo shoot	20 g, finely chopped
Corn flour (cornstarch)	a pinch

Seasoning (to taste)

Salt

Sugar

Ground white pepper

Sesame oil

Chilli oil

Soei gau dough

Plain (all-purpose) flour	600 g
Salt	a pinch
Water	300 ml
Corn flour (cornstarch)	115 g

Dumplings in Superior Stock
Sheung Tong Soei Gau 上汤水饺

These dumplings are fashioned after the rustic northern Chinese dumplings, so the skins are thicker and the filling is coarser than the Cantonese variety.

Method

- Prepare filling. Combine filling ingredients except corn flour. Add seasoning to taste then add corn flour to bind lightly. Set aside.

- Prepare *soei gau* dough. Mix flour, salt and water together to form a dough. Roll out on a floured surface into a cylinder. Divide into 24 equal pieces.

- Roll each dough piece out into a thin, round skin. Dust skins with corn flour to prevent sticking.

- Spoon some filling onto each skin. Fold skin over into a half moon to enclose filling. Press edges to seal.

- Cook dumplings in superior stock.

- Add yellow chives and season soup to taste with salt, sesame oil and chilli oil before serving.

Note: The classic superior stock is made from boiling Chinese ham, chicken bones and pork bones. Alternatively, you may want to use prawn shells instead of Chinese ham, as some restaurants in Hong Kong do when they prepare their stock. The flavour will, however, not be as delicate as that of the classic superior stock.

MAKES 1

Ingredients

Glutinous rice	60 g, washed, soaked overnight and drained
Cooking oil	
Spring onion (scallion)	1, chopped
Ginger	1-cm knob, peeled and chopped
Garlic	2 cloves, peeled and chopped
Dried prawns (shrimps)	1 Tbsp, soaked overnight and drained
Fatty pork	40 g
Split green beans	20 g
Chestnuts	2, peeled
Salted egg yolk	1
Dried Chinese mushroom	1, soaked to soften and squeezed dry
Dried lotus leaf	1

Seasoning (to taste)

Five spice powder
Salt
Sugar
Sesame oil
Ground white pepper

Glutinous Rice Dumpling
Guo Zeng Zong 裹蒸棕

Method

- Mix glutinous rice with seasoning to taste. Set aside.
- Heat some oil and sauté spring onion, ginger and garlic until fragrant. Add dried prawns and pork. Sauté until fragrant.
- Spread half the glutinous rice on the lotus leaf, followed by half the split green beans and sautéed ingredients. Top with chestnuts, salted egg yolk and mushroom. Cover with remaining split green beans then remaining glutinous rice. Fold leaf into a parcel, leaving some room for the glutinous rice to expand. Secure with string.
- Immerse in boiling water and cook for 3–4 hours.
- Serve with sugar and/or dark soy sauce.

MAKES 8

Ingredients

Lamb	200 g, diced by hand
Coriander (cilantro)	1 sprig, diced
Spring onions (scallions)	1, diced
Garlic	3 cloves, peeled and diced

Seasoning (to taste)

Sesame oil
Chinese *hua tiao* wine
Salt
Sugar
Ground white pepper

Dough

Plain (all-purpose) flour	300 g
Water	130 ml or as needed

Pan-baked Bread
Loh Paeng 烙饼

This recipe is inspired by the rustic street foods of northern China. It reflects a very casual style of cooking where bread dough is simply slapped on a hot pan to cook. Though the bread is unevenly charred at parts, it is fragrant.

Method

- Mix lamb with coriander, spring onions and garlic. Add seasoning to taste.
- Mix flour with enough water to form a dough. Roll dough out on a floured surface into a cylinder and divide into 8 equal pieces.
- Roll each dough piece out into a thin, round skin. Dust each piece lightly with flour to prevent it from sticking to the pan later. Spread some lamb mixture over.
- Heat a pan until evenly hot. Place dough into pan to cook, without oil, until browned at parts. Flip over to cook other side. Serve hot.

Notes: As an alternative, you can also cook the lamb topping and bread separately. Sauté the lamb mixture with a little oil until cooked then set aside. Cook bread in a dry pan then spoon lamb topping on bread to serve.

MAKES 10–12 BOWLS

Ingredients

Black sesame seeds	200 g
Water	1.5 litres
Yellow (step) sugar (*peen tong*)	230 g

Black Sesame Paste

Zi Ma Wu 芝麻湖

Method

- Pan-fry black sesame seeds until fragrant. Grind with water and sugar to get a paste.
- Cook paste over very low heat, stirring gently, for 15–20 minutes. Serve hot.

Note: Do not cook the black sesame paste over high heat as it will dry out and the taste will not be as smooth.

MAKES AN 18 X 18-CM TRAY

Ingredients

Sugar cane juice	600 ml
Gelatine powder	2¹/₂ tsp
Sugar	to taste

Sugar Cane Jelly
Zeh Zap Leung Gou 蔗汁涼糕

Method

- Combine ingredients in a pot and bring to the boil.
- Strain mixture into a 18 x 18-cm tray. Allow to cool then chill in the refrigerator until firm.
- Cut into bite-sized pieces and garnish with fruits as preferred.

Note:
- Buy freshly squeezed sugar cane juice without the ice. I prefer to use the juice of green sugar cane instead of the darker, brownish varieties. Green sugar cane has a lighter, more delicate flavour.
- This jelly is best enjoyed as an accompaniment to a rich Chinese-style pastry. I would also recommend serving it on a light-coloured plate to play up its pretty green hue.

MAKES 10 BOWLS

Ingredients

Green beans	150 g, soaked overnight
Rue (*chau chou*)	10 g
Raw peanuts (groundnuts)	75 g
Water	
Sago pearls	30 g
Yellow (step) sugar (*peen tong*)	to taste

Sweet Green Bean Peanut Dessert
Lok Tau Sar 绿豆沙

The texture of this classic sweet soup should be floury with coarsely broken beans.

Method

- Drain green beans and discard any skin that has been shed.
- Combine green beans, rue and peanuts in a clay pot and add enough water to cover them. Simmer over low heat for 2–3 hours until peanuts are soft. Add more water as it evaporates.
- Add sago pearls 20 minutes before end of cooking time. Stir sugar in 5 minutes before the end of cooking time.
- Serve hot.

Note:

Rue is a type of herb commonly used for this dish. It is available at Chinese grocery stores.

To shorten the cooking time, you can pre-steam the green beans and peanuts, although the fragrance of the final dish may be compromised.

MAKES 12 BOWLS

Ingredients

Sweet almonds (*narm harn*)	600 g, soaked overnight and drained
Bitter almonds (*pak harn*)	150 g, soaked overnight and drained
Water	1 litre
Sugar	to taste
Quail eggs	12

Almond Tea with Quail Eggs
Jeok Dan Harn Yarn Cha 崔旦杏仁茶

Method

- Grind almonds together with water to form a paste. Add more water if mixture appears too thick.

- Strain mixture and discard pulp. Use only the juice although you can leave a little bit of the finely ground pulp in, if preferred.

- Bring almond juice and sugar to a gentle boil, stirring constantly.

- Remove from heat, ladle into individual serving bowls and crack a quail egg into each bowl. Serve immediately.

Note:

- It is important not to boil the almond juice too vigorously as it will become very foamy.

- As a variation to this recipe, you can stir in egg white, ground walnuts, Sichuan fritillary bulb (*chuan bei*), fresh milk or ground rice when cooking the almond mixture.

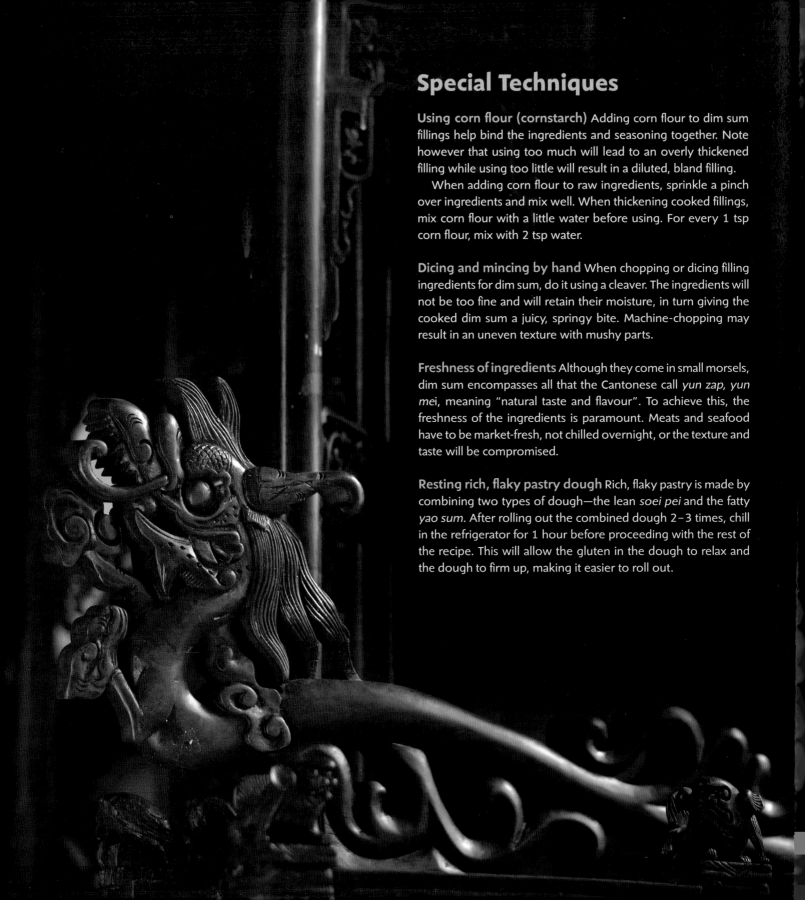

Special Techniques

Using corn flour (cornstarch) Adding corn flour to dim sum fillings help bind the ingredients and seasoning together. Note however that using too much will lead to an overly thickened filling while using too little will result in a diluted, bland filling.

When adding corn flour to raw ingredients, sprinkle a pinch over ingredients and mix well. When thickening cooked fillings, mix corn flour with a little water before using. For every 1 tsp corn flour, mix with 2 tsp water.

Dicing and mincing by hand When chopping or dicing filling ingredients for dim sum, do it using a cleaver. The ingredients will not be too fine and will retain their moisture, in turn giving the cooked dim sum a juicy, springy bite. Machine-chopping may result in an uneven texture with mushy parts.

Freshness of ingredients Although they come in small morsels, dim sum encompasses all that the Cantonese call *yun zap, yun mei*, meaning "natural taste and flavour". To achieve this, the freshness of the ingredients is paramount. Meats and seafood have to be market-fresh, not chilled overnight, or the texture and taste will be compromised.

Resting rich, flaky pastry dough Rich, flaky pastry is made by combining two types of dough—the lean *soei pei* and the fatty *yao sum*. After rolling out the combined dough 2–3 times, chill in the refrigerator for 1 hour before proceeding with the rest of the recipe. This will allow the gluten in the dough to relax and the dough to firm up, making it easier to roll out.

Glossary

Alkaline water (*garn soei*) Also know as lye water, this is used in very small quantities to give cakes such as Sweet Potato Cake (*Kam Xu Ma Lai Gou*) on pg 53 a smooth and springy texture.

Almonds There are two types of almonds—sweet (*narm harn*) and bitter (*pak harn*). Bitter almonds relieve coughing and chest pains while sweet almonds are rich in protein and nourish the skin. Raw bitter almonds contain traces of toxins, so cook thoroughly and use only in small quantities. Consult the Chinese herbalist if unsure.

Ammonia powder (*chow fun*) This powder produces a strong alkaline reaction when used. The Sugar-crusted Buns with Fresh Pineapple Filling (*Po Loh Bao*) on pg 119 uses it to lighten its flaky crust.

Bamboo shoot This is the young shoot of the bamboo. Fresh bamboo shoot requires lengthy preparation, but canned bamboo shoot is available from the supermarkets and is ready-to-use.

Dried vegetables (*choi gorn*) This salted, dried Chinese cabbage and is widely available at Chinese grocery stores. It is usually added to soups and porridge for its 'cooling' effect.

Dumpling/spring roll/*siew mai*/*wan tan* skin An assortment of ready-made skins are widely available at the frozen section of supermarkets. Spring roll skins are white in colour. They are cooked and contain no egg. Those sold in the supermarkets are usually square in shape while the freshly made ones are round. *Siew mai* skins are yellow in colour. They are made with egg and are similar to *wan tan* skin, but for their shape. *Siew mai* skins are round, while *wan tan* skins are square.

Flours The flour's gluten, or protein content, governs how weak or strong the flour is and consequently affects the texture and elasticity of the dough. Plain (all-purpose) flour has a medium-gluten content of about 10 per cent. Medium-gluten flour is known as *zong garn fun* in Cantonese.

High-gluten flour (also known as bread flour or strong flour) or *gou garn fun* in Cantonese, is used for chewy buns, breads and noodles. It has a protein (gluten) content of about 12 per cent. Dough made using high-gluten flour is elastic and strong.

Low-gluten (or weak) flour, *dai garn fan* in Cantonese, produces fluffy, spongy cakes and breads. Flours labelled as "cake flour" have a lower gluten content than plain flour, and would be suitable for use where low-gluten flour is called for. Flours with even lower gluten content are available. Check with baking supplies shops.

Haw flakes (*san zha*) These reddish coloured sweet-sour flakes are sold as sweets and snacks. They are available as small discs from supermarkets. Haw flakes are made from the hawthorn fruit which is believed to aid digestion.

Instant dried yeast This yeast comes in fine grains. It is called "instant" because it does not require prior rehydration before being added to flour. The grains will dissolve quickly into the dough as it is mixed. It keeps well if stored in a cold, dry place.

Lotus seed paste This is a sweet, thick paste made from mashing lotus seeds with sugar and oil. It is available at most baking supplies shops.

Olive seeds (*larm yarn*) Also known as olive nuts, these are the beige-coloured seed/kernel of white Chinese olives. They are small and oval in shape, much like pine nuts which they are often substituted for.

Red bean paste This deep-red, almost black sweet paste is made from mashing red beans with sugar and oil. Like Lotus seed paste, it is available at baking supplies shops.

Red fermented bean curd This bean curd is pickled with chillies, spices, lemon juice and fermented red rice. It has a strong flavour and creamy texture.

Kingsford's corn flour (cornstarch) (*yin sok fun*) This brand of corn flour is high in quality. It is used to thicken sauces and coat ingredients before cooking.

Torch ginger bud This is the pink flower bud of the ginger plant. Its petals are very aromatic and are usually used raw to flavour dishes.

Wheat starch flour (*dung meen fun*) This is the by-product when the protein has been removed from wheat to make gluten. Wheat starch flour is commonly used to make the dough for crystal- or translucent-skinned dim sum.

Starter dough (*bao zong*) A starter dough is made by mixing yeast, flour and water then leaving it covered in a warm place to ferment. Once it ferments, becoming bubbly and smelling sour and yeasty, it is ready for use.

Restaurants usually make a larger portion, the remainder of which is constantly replenished by regular, scheduled additions of flour and water, so the dough is always ready when needed. Over time, the dough will become more stable and sour, adding flavour and texture to breads.

The first batch of breads that you make using new starter dough may not be as flavoursome as you would have hoped. But the longer the starter dough has been maintained, the better will be the flavour and texture of the breads that are made using it.

Starter Dough *Bao Zong*

Ingredients

Flour*	600 g
Instant dried yeast	1 tsp
White vinegar	1 Tbsp
Water from rinsing rice	250 ml

*For the best results, use high-gluten flour for fried or baked breads and low-gluten flour for steamed breads. Medium-gluten flour can be used for fried, baked or steamed breads.

Method

- Mix ingredients into dough and leave at room temperature for 24 hours, covered with a piece of cloth. It should become foamy and smell sour and yeasty. Use as indicated in recipe, but leave 50 g of starter dough behind for future use.

- For every 50 g starter dough left behind, replenish by mixing in 600 g flour and 300 ml water. Leave to ferment for 12 hours until foamy and yeasty before use.

- If you're not planning to use the starter dough within the next 24 hours, refrigerate it. It will keep for up to 2 months.

- To use, remove from refrigerator a day ahead. Leave at room temperature from morning until mid afternoon. Replenish with 600 g flour and 300 ml water for every 50 g starter dough. Allow to ferment until needed.

Superior stock (*sheung tong*) This golden-hued stock is made from boiling choice ingredients such as Chinese ham, fresh whole chicken, chunks of pork and whole pork bones.

Superior Stock *Sheung Tong*

MAKES 4 LITRES

Ingredients

Good quality Chinese ham (eg. Jinghua ham)	500 g
Chicken	1.5 kg
Whole pork bones	1 kg
Lean pork	1.5 kg
Orange peel	1–2 slices
Water	

Method

- Place all ingredients, except orange peel, in a pot. Add enough water to cover ingredients and bring to the boil. Allow it to boil for 1 minute. Drain and rinse ingredients.

- Add orange peel and enough water to cover ingredients, and bring to the boil again. Lower heat and simmer, partially covered, for 3–4 hours, skimming off any scum that surfaces.

- Allow to cool then strain stock. Use as needed. The stock be can refrigerated for up to 4 days or kept frozen for up to 3 months.

- The meats can be returned to the pot, with more water, and boiled for 2 hours to produce *yee tong* or "number 2 stock". It will be less concentrated than *sheung tong* and can be used in general cooking.

- Another more luxurious stock is *ting tong* which is made by simmering superior stock with a new batch of ingredients to get an even more deeply golden, fragrant and concentrated stock. This expensive and time-consuming stock is usually reserved for making shark's fin and bird's nest soups.

Cooking Utensils

1. Pastry cutter This is similar to a pizza cutter. It is generally used for cutting and trimming rolled-out dough to size.

2. Dough scraper This handy piece of plastic is used for scraping dough off a work surface. It is also used to cut dough into small pieces.

3. Pastry brush This brush is used for greasing baking tins and pans, and also for glazing the top of pastries with beaten egg for a shiny, golden finish.

4. Rolling pin, slim This slim, wooden rolling pin is used to roll out small portions of dough into thin skins or wrappers. Wood is the preferred material as it traps a fine layer of flour, making the rolling out of dough easier.

5. Rolling pin, large A heavy rolling pin is generally used to roll out large blocks of dough to get sheets of regular thickness.

6. Palette spatula This wooden tool is useful for scraping up small portions of dumpling filling and pressing it into the hand cupping the dumpling skin. If unavailable, a teaspoon works as well.

7. Round cutters These come in various sizes and are used to cut out rounds of dough or pastry.

8. *Har Gau* Cleaver (*har gau tou*) This broad cleaver is specially made for flattening out dim sum doughs into thin, round skins. The edge of this thin-bladed cleaver is blunt, which makes it safer to use. It can be found at shops selling Chinese utensils. Ask for *har gau tou* ("*tou*" meaning "knife"). To use, grease a broad side of the cleaver then press it, greased side down, onto the dough. Turn the blade in a clockwise direction to flatten dough into a half circle then turn the blade in an anti-clockwise direction to get a thin, round skin.

9. Old-fashioned scale This small weighing instrument is still widely used in restaurants. It is usually used to measure tiny quantities of ingredients such as baking powder, yeast and sugar. It is sensitive to quantities as small as 1 tsin which is around 3.8 g.

Weights & Measures

Quantities for this book are given in Metric and American (spoon and cup) measures. Standard spoon and cup measurements used are: 1 tsp = 5 ml, 1 Tbsp = 15 ml, 1 cup = 250 ml. All measures are level unless otherwise stated.

LIQUID AND VOLUME MEASURES

Metric	Imperial	American
5 ml	$^1/_6$ fl oz	1 teaspoon
10 ml	$^1/_3$ fl oz	1 dessertspoon
15 ml	$^1/_2$ fl oz	1 tablespoon
60 ml	2 fl oz	$^1/_4$ cup (4 tablespoons)
85 ml	$2^1/_2$ fl oz	$^1/_3$ cup
90 ml	3 fl oz	$^3/_8$ cup (6 tablespoons)
125 ml	4 fl oz	$^1/_2$ cup
180 ml	6 fl oz	$^3/_4$ cup
250 ml	8 fl oz	1 cup
300 ml	10 fl oz ($^1/_2$ pint)	$1^1/_4$ cups
375 ml	12 fl oz	$1^1/_2$ cups
435 ml	14 fl oz	$1^3/_4$ cups
500 ml	16 fl oz	2 cups
625 ml	20 fl oz (1 pint)	$2^1/_2$ cups
750 ml	24 fl oz ($1^1/_5$ pints)	3 cups
1 litre	32 fl oz ($1^3/_5$ pints)	4 cups
1.25 litres	40 fl oz (2 pints)	5 cups
1.5 litres	48 fl oz ($2^2/_5$ pints)	6 cups
2.5 litres	80 fl oz (4 pints)	10 cups

DRY MEASURES

Metric	Imperial
30 grams	1 ounce
45 grams	$1^1/_2$ ounces
55 grams	2 ounces
70 grams	$2^1/_2$ ounces
85 grams	3 ounces
100 grams	$3^1/_2$ ounces
110 grams	4 ounces
125 grams	$4^1/_2$ ounces
140 grams	5 ounces
280 grams	10 ounces
450 grams	16 ounces (1 pound)
500 grams	1 pound, $1^1/_2$ ounces
700 grams	$1^1/_2$ pounds
800 grams	$1^3/_4$ pounds
1 kilogram	2 pounds, 3 ounces
1.5 kilograms	3 pounds, $4^1/_2$ ounces
2 kilograms	4 pounds, 6 ounces

LENGTH

Metric	Imperial
0.5 cm	$^1/_4$ inch
1 cm	$^1/_2$ inch
1.5 cm	$^3/_4$ inch
2.5 cm	1 inch

OVEN TEMPERATURE

	°C	°F	Gas Regulo	
Very slow	120	250	1	
Slow	150	300	2	
Moderately slow	160	325	3	
Moderate	180	350	4	
Moderately hot	190/200	370/400	5/6	
Hot	210/220	410/440	6/7	
Very hot	230	450	8	
Super hot	250/290	475/550	9/10	

ABBREVIATION

tsp	teaspoon
Tbsp	tablespoon
g	gram
kg	kilogram
ml	millilitre